EGGS IN THE KITCHEN

EGGS IN THE KITCHEN

THE ESSENTIAL GUIDE TO PREPARING AND COOKING EGGS

ALEX BARKER

LORENZ BOOKS

This edition is published by Lorenz Books, an imprint of Anness Publishing Ltd,
108 Great Russell Street, London WC1B 3NA; info@anness.com

www.lorenzbooks.com; www.annesspublishing.com

If you like the images in this book and would like to investigate using them for publishing, promotions or
advertising, please visit our website www.practicalpictures.com for more information.

Publisher: Joanna Lorenz
Editor: Susannah Blake
Copy Editor: Bridget Jones
Indexer: Hilary Bird
Designer: Nigel Partridge
Photography: Amanda Heywood (recipes) and Steve Moss (reference section)
Food for Photography: Joy Skipper (recipes) and
Alex Barker and Stephanie England (reference section)
Production Controller: Pirong Wang

PUBLISHER'S NOTE
Although the advice and information in this book are believed to be accurate and true at the time of
going to press, neither the authors nor the publisher can accept any legal responsibility or liability for any
errors or omissions that may have been made nor for any inaccuracies nor for any loss, harm or injury
that comes about from following instructions or advice in this book.

NOTES
Bracketed terms are intended for American readers.
For all recipes, quantities are given in both metric and imperial measures and,
where appropriate, in standard cups and spoons. Follow one set of measures, but not a mixture,
because they are not interchangeable.
Standard spoon and cup measures are level. 1 tsp = 5ml, 1 tbsp = 15ml, 1 cup = 250ml/8fl oz.
Australian standard tablespoons are 20ml. Australian readers should use 3 tsp in place of 1 tbsp for
measuring small quantities.
American pints are 16fl oz/2 cups. American readers should use 20fl oz/2.5 cups in place of
1 pint when measuring liquids.
Electric oven temperatures in this book are for conventional ovens. When using a fan oven, the
temperature will probably need to be reduced by about 10–20°C/20–40°F. Since ovens vary, you should
check with your manufacturer's instruction book for guidance.
Medium (US large) eggs are used unless otherwise stated.
The very young, the elderly, pregnant women and those in ill-health or with a compromised immune system
are advised against consuming raw eggs or dishes and drinks containing raw eggs.

CONTENTS

INTRODUCTION

Egyptian and Chinese records show that fowl were laying eggs for man as early as 1400BC and the use of eggs in the kitchen has been noted since Greek and Roman times.

Chickens reared today are thought to have descended from the Red Jungle Fowl *Gallus*, a native of the Himalayas some 4,000 years ago. The birds were probably brought to Europe from Asia and were then taken to America by Christopher Columbus in 1493. By the 14th century, several types of eggs were being eaten, including those from the duck, goose, plover, seagull and a short-legged hen called a "creepie", which laid very small eggs.

In the Middle Ages, eggs were often poached, posing an interesting problem for those eating with fingers and sharing plates. However, from early records, one

Below: Poultry have been domesticated and farmed for their eggs for centuries.

of the most popular ways of cooking eggs was in the ashes of a softwood fire. John Cardy Jeaffreson, a late 19th-century author on social history, included the following quotation in *A Book About the Table*, published in 1875: "The peasant who bakes his egg in hot wood embers piled about the shell, knows by a sure sign when the meat is sufficiently cooked. As soon as a clear dew-drop exudes from the shell's top, visible above the embers, the egg is done to the perfection of softness."

In total contrast, by the time Jeaffreson was writing on the history of egg cooking, eggs were in use in lavish dishes in the Victorian kitchen. Mrs Beeton, the famous author of the *Book of Cookery and Household Management*, wrote that every good cook needs "an ample sufficiency of eggs with cream and new milk". It was the Victorians who introduced the idea of eating eggs for breakfast. Whatever else was eaten,

Above: Throughout history, eggs have been considered as a source of food. This 13th-century manuscript depicts a group of women buying eggs.

in genteel households, each morning the cook would coddle a cluster of fresh eggs in an elaborate china hen to greet the family when they sat down to breakfast. Trays taken to those who opted for breakfast in the privacy of their bed chambers included eggs nestling under cosies – thick woollen coats designed to retain the heat, not the dainty egg cosies we know today.

Throughout history, eggs have been associated with the universe, creation and new life. The Egyptians believed that their God, Ptah, created the egg out of the sun and the moon and the Phoenicians thought that two halves of a very large egg had split open to produce heaven and earth. Similarly, in Chinese legend, the universe was egg-shaped, with the yolk representing the earth and the white the heavens. Early man separated the yolk from the white, introducing the idea of the white, the clear element, as yang and the yolk, the dark murky earth, as yin. To the Chinese, the egg is a symbol of fertility, so when a child is born the parents give dyed eggs as gifts to friends.

Because of its connection with new life, the egg has often been thought of as an aphrodisiac and a fertility aid. In

Above, clockwise from top left: Bantam eggs, hen's eggs, pullet's eggs, quail's eggs and white hen's eggs

Central Europe, farmers would rub eggs on their ploughs hoping to improve the crops and in France, brides would break an egg on the doorstep of their new home to ensure a large family.

Egg painting is an art around the world. In Japan eggs are painted red as tokens of luck and joy. Coloured eggs often feature in Jewish and Middle Eastern religious festivals. Jewish *haminodos* are baked with onions or saffron until they are rich golden, rust or red in colour. One traditional recipe for these shiny exotic eggs runs as follows. "Mix equal proportions olive oil and Turkish coffee. Put in this mixture as many eggs as requested, in their shells, and cook them on a very slow fire for twelve hours. The mixture will penetrate the shells, give the white an

amber colour, the yolks the colour of saffron, and the eggs will have the taste of the most delicious chestnuts you have ever eaten."

For centuries, eggs have had a religious or spiritual significance attached to them. To the early Egyptians, Persians, Romans and Greeks, the egg was symbolic of the universe and continuing life and represented the sun of spring. Eggs

have long been associated with new life at Easter after the fasting of Lent. In Mediterranean countries, sweet Easter breads, such as Greek *tsoureki*, are baked and adorned with brightly painted or dyed eggs, and chocolate eggs, although a modern addition to Easter celebrations, are also popular. Similar associations between life and fertility are made in Judaism, during the Passover celebrations.

Eggs are not only eaten at Easter but they also feature in traditional seasonal games. Easter egg hunts; egg tapping, sometimes a very messy game; and egg rolling, usually ending with a race down a hill or across a garden, are just a few examples. These and other games are part of the annual Easter festivities attended by the President at the White House in the United States of America.

Left: Egg painting has long been a tradition in many cultures.

THE STRUCTURE OF THE EGG

The shell Hens today produce eggs that are two or three times larger than those produced by their ancestors. Surprisingly, the actual amount of shell has not increased, resulting in eggs with a much thinner, more delicate shell. Luckily, with domesticated hens, the shell is no longer needed to protect the chick from would-be aggressors. The egg shell makes up 12 per cent of the total weight of the egg and is composed largely of calcium. Its strength is influenced by the hen's diet and age. Larger hens produce larger eggs with thinner shells. The shell is porous, allowing moisture out and air in, which is vital for the early development of the chick. The shell is also covered with a protective coating, which helps to prevent bacteria entering the egg.

The air cell The inside of the shell is lined with two very thin membranes. At the rounded end of the egg, the membranes separate slightly to produce a space that is filled with air. As the egg ages, moisture and carbon dioxide pass through the pores of the shell and are replaced by more air, which collects in the space. As the air cell grows, the egg becomes lighter and will eventually float if placed in a glass of water.

The white This is the albumen and it makes up about 67 per cent of the egg's total weight. It is transluscent when uncooked and contains over half of the protein found in an egg. It is thicker immediately around a fresh yolk while the outer part of the white is thinner. As the egg ages, the distinction between these two layers of white diminishes. Twisted strands run through the white to anchor the yolk in place. These are the chalazae and the more prominent they are, the fresher the egg. Although the chalazae do not affect the cooking qualities of the egg, you may prefer to strain them out of custards and sauces as they can set in fine strings that spoil the eating quality of smooth mixtures.

Below: The colour of an egg's shell is determined solely by the breed of bird.

The yolk Surrounded by a membrane, the yolk makes up about a third of the egg. It contains all the fat, just less than half the protein, all the vitamins A, D and E and most of the minerals that can be found in an egg. The colour of the yolk depends purely on the diet of a hen. A diet rich in yellow corn will produce medium-yellow yolks. Natural foods colours, such as nasturtiums, can be added to produce the popular rich yellow colour. Yolks occasionally have blood spots on them and, although unsightly, are just a sign of freshness and do not indicate that the egg has been fertilized. If you find these spots unappetizing, they can be removed very easily before cooking.

THE NUTRITIONAL VALUE OF EGGS

Often referred to as the most complete and pure food, eggs contain everything needed for the growth of the young chick and this also provides a very good source of food for humans. Eggs are primarily a protein food, and the protein they provide contains all eight amino acids that are essential for growth and repair of the body. Because it is of such high quality, egg protein is used as the standard by which to measure the value of other protein foods. One medium (US large) egg will provide 12–14 per cent of the recommended daily allowance of protein for an adult.

An egg contains fat in the yolk, but it is not a high-fat food. A medium egg yolk contains about 1.6g fat, just over 50 per cent of which is unsaturated, with 29 per cent saturated fatty acids.

Eggs contain varying amounts of 13 vitamins, most importantly vitamins D, A and E and many of the B vitamins. However, eggs do not contain any vitamin C.

Eggs are also a useful source of minerals, including phosphorus, iron and calcium, and the essential trace elements zinc, iodine and selenium. The amount of calcium is small, with a medium egg providing about 3 per cent of the daily recommended intake.

The energy provided by an egg varies from 66Kcals/276kJ for a small egg to 94Kcals/394kJ for a very large egg.

Above: There is no difference in the nutritional value of white or brown eggs.

HANDLING EGGS

Eggs should be stored at a constant temperature, preferably below 8°C/46.5°F. Hands, work surfaces and equipment should be cleaned thoroughly after cooking with eggs to prevent potential contamination of bacteria from eggs to other foods that may be eaten raw.

WHITE VERSUS BROWN

There is no difference in the nutritional value of white or brown eggs. The colour of the shell is determined by the breed of hen. Breeds with white feathers and ear lobes, such as Leghorn, lay white eggs. Breeds with red feathers and red ear lobes, such as Rhode Island Red or Plymouth Rock, lay brown eggs. White eggs are preferred in the United States, with a few exceptions, including New England, where brown eggs are more popular. The colour of the yolk is influenced by diet, and feed that is high in corn will result in very yellow egg yolks.

DOUBLE THE VALUE

Double-yolked eggs are the result of two egg cells maturing at the same time. The two cells pass through the hen's reproductive system together and are surrounded by a single white and shell. They are usually produced by young hens whose reproductive cycles are not fully synchronized.

Below: Occasionally, you may find an egg that contains two yolks within a single white.

CHOLESTEROL

This fat-like substance is produced naturally in the body and found in the blood. It is essential for body cells, digestive juices and hormones, but the body can have too much. Cholesterol is found in egg yolk, but not in the white. If you are on a low-fat diet, particularly to help control blood cholesterol levels, you should limit egg consumption to no more than one a day.

SALMONELLA

These bacteria are found in poultry and on the surface of other raw meats. They can cause severe food poisoning if they are present in high numbers when food is eaten. Although infected hens can contaminate eggs, recently instigated quality controls have reduced this risk. Careful handling, rigorous inspection and control of all sources of raw meat are measures now in place. Imported products are also subject to tight control, especially those from countries that have poor contamination records. Constant storage at or below 20°C/68°F is enforced to prevent bacteria from multiplying. The Lion code of practice used in the UK is being adopted by other countries, so all young hens that are bred for egg production are vaccinated against salmonella.

It is generally recommended that raw eggs should not be served to the very young, the elderly or to those in ill-health or with a compromised immune system. Thoroughly cooking eggs at a temperature above 60°C/140°F will ensure that bacteria are killed off. Eggs can sometimes be lightly cooked for use in recipes that traditionally use raw eggs. Meringues can be made using a hot syrup, whisked over hot water, and yolks can be heated very gently with a minimum of 30ml/2 tbsp liquid per yolk, stirring continuously, until the mixture coats the back of a spoon or reaches a temperature of 71°C/160°F.

Choosing, Using and Cooking with Eggs

When people think of eggs they think of the hen's eggs included in their weekly shopping. However, there are many other, more unusual varieties that are becoming more readily available, such as pheasant and guinea fowl eggs, or even gull's eggs. This chapter gives fascinating information on the types of eggs available, their appearance and flavour, and advice on where to buy them and how to store them. There is also invaluable guidance on how to test the freshness of an egg, its cooking properties, and the range of cooking equipment available to achieve great results.

VARIETIES OF EGGS

Hen's eggs are part of the regular diet for most of the world's population and there are many countries that regard any eggs as a source of food. Third World countries and areas with large peasant populations, particularly where food is scarce, still regard any form of protein food as very important. Eggs from the blackbird, fulmar, gannet, guillemot, gull, penguin, plover, puffin, swan, thrush and more are all eaten. In some parts of the world, any nest that can be reached is a potential source of food. Many stories tell of the delicious nature of wild birds' eggs. In countries that do not suffer food shortages, collecting wild birds' eggs is now illegal as, with a few exceptions, wild or game birds' eggs are protected.

Below: Contented Rhode Island Reds peck their way around the farmyard.

Even the most unlikely eggs are a delicacy to some gourmets, as the following description reveals. "Penguins' eggs are laid in holes in the ground on the little Guano Islands off the coast of South Africa, they are delicious when perfectly fresh, plain hard boiled and cold; they much resemble plovers' eggs in taste and texture and are equal in bulk to about three of the latter."

Of course it is not only birds' eggs that are eaten. Turtle eggs are a delicacy around the many islands of the Pacific and the warmer parts of the Atlantic, where they are considered to be an aphrodisiac; they are also a prized ingredient in Asian cooking. Round, white and shaped like ping-pong balls, turtle eggs are soft-shelled and delicious baked in bamboo leaves over the fire. They are a treat local inhabitants might occasionally allow

themselves, though they would never take more than a few eggs from the nest at any time. Poachers, on the other hand, are not as scrupulous and have endangered the species by lying in wait for the female turtle to lay anything up to 200 eggs in a night in sandy hollows above the water line, before they take all the eggs. International laws are now in place to prevent this profiteering and to counteract the destruction of the life cycle of the turtle. Other reptile eggs are also enjoyed in Asia.

Fish eggs are highly prized. Sturgeon eggs, known as caviar, are the most famous and expensive. These shiny black, salty eggs are adored by the Russians and cost a small fortune per teaspoonful. Shiny red salmon eggs, also known as caviar, are less expensive and have become fashionable, mainly for their colour.

Above: When available, bantam eggs are a good choice for young children because of their small size.

HEN'S EGGS

These eggs are produced by the billion each year. Domesticated hens are the most prolific producers of eggs for culinary use around the world. Of the many hundreds of breeds of hen, only a handful are actually reared for commercial egg production. The breed has to be chosen for the specific environment in which it is to be reared and for the eggs it lays, as they must be suitable for selling. Cross-breeds from the popular Rhode Island Red, such as Isabrown, Hy-Line and Babcock, are the source of the majority of commercial eggs, but small farms and specialist breeders sometimes rear some of the more romantically named hens, such as Black Maran, Brahma, Indian Game, Buff Orpington, Plymouth Rock and Silkie. Silkies produce very small dainty

Right: A medium hen's egg weighs about 50g/2oz.

Above: Eggs vary in size and colour, depending on the breed of bird.

white eggs, which are good for baking and for children's meals. Rhode Island Reds are excellent layers and produce the classic light brown egg. Other breeds, such as Marans, lay speckled, deep tan to dark brown eggs, while Araucanas lay eggs that are a very pale blue.

BANTAM EGGS

Being about half the size of hens, bantams produce much smaller eggs. In some cases, bantams are natural dwarf animals or they may be specially bred miniatures of the larger breeds. Their eggs have a similar flavour to hen's eggs and can be used in the same way as full-size eggs, but you will need to double the number of eggs required in the recipe. Bantams are kept by small or specialist farmers, so their eggs are not widely available. They can sometimes be found in farm stores.

Left: A bantam egg is about half the size of a hen's egg.

Above: Quail's eggs are valued for their appearance as well as their flavour.

QUAIL'S EGGS

These tiny eggs are about one-third of the size of hen's eggs and are readily available in stores and supermarkets. They are the smallest of all commercial eggs. They have dark-speckled, pale shells and make an attractive garnish when served in the half shell. The shelled eggs are also excellent in appetizers and canapés, or as a garnish. If they are not overcooked by boiling until too hard, they have a light, almost creamy texture and flavour. Quail's eggs can be poached and cooked in the same way as hen's eggs.

DUCK EGGS

Domesticated ducks originated from wild waterfowl. Their eggs are bigger than hen's eggs, weighing about 90g/3½oz, and their shell colour can vary from shades of very pale green-blue to white. They have a slightly higher fat content and oilier texture than hen's eggs. They are richer in flavour,

Left: A tiny quail's egg weighs about 20g/¾oz.

which makes them ideal for baking, but the whites are firmer and slightly rubbery in texture when set, so they are not to everyone's taste when plainly cooked. Their rich yellow yolks produce wonderfully golden sponges but the whites are unsuitable for meringues.

Duck eggs are often laid in muddy places, so they should be always be washed and thoroughly cooked. A

Right: A duck egg is about the same size as a very large hen's egg.

boiling time of at least 10 minutes is recommended. These eggs are available mainly from speciality food stores, butchers, fishmongers and delicatessens. They should be stored in the refrigerator and eaten as soon as possible. For a better result, allow duck eggs to return to room temperature before cooking.

Left: Duck eggs come in translucent shades of blue, green and white.

Below: Domesticated ducks can be very good layers.

GOOSE EGGS

Geese are notorious for being unfriendly and extremely noisy and are sometimes said to be a good alternative to guard dogs. Their eggs are at least twice the size of hen's eggs, weighing about 200g/7oz each, and are a pure, chalky white. The shells of goose eggs are usually very hard. Geese are fairly messy birds so, like duck eggs, goose eggs need washing and thorough cooking to kill any harmful bacteria that may be lurking on their shells.

Although they are stronger in flavour than hen's eggs, goose eggs are slightly milder than duck eggs and are not as rich. They can be cooked simply and eaten on their own, but they are particularly good as an ingredient in mildly flavoured baked dishes, such as vegetable gratins and quiches.

Goose eggs are available in season from specialist butchers, delicatessens and farm stores.

Left: Geese are well-known for their aggressive nature so it is a good idea to keep a safe distance.

Below: The shells of goose eggs are pure white and very hard.

Below: A goose egg is twice the size of a hen's egg and weighs about 200g/7oz.

Above and below: Turkey eggs are slightly larger than hen's eggs and have an attractive speckled shell.

Above: Guinea fowl eggs are a similar size to bantam eggs and weigh about 25g/1oz each.

GUINEA FOWL EGGS

These birds are related to pheasants and chickens. Their eggs are roughly half the size of hen's eggs and weigh about 25g/1oz each. They are light brown and very regular in colour. Guinea fowl eggs have a light and delicate flavour. They are ideal for garnishing dishes or adding to salads and are also good for baking. They are available from specialist breeders.

TURKEY EGGS

These eggs weigh about 75g/3oz and have creamy white shells with light brown speckles. The smaller eggs of young birds tend to be paler than those of older birds. Although turkeys are farmed in most parts of the world, their eggs are rarely available. The birds are usually bred for their meat so their eggs are kept for hatching. However, outside the main breeding season you may find a local farmer who has some to spare. There is little difference in taste between turkey and hen's eggs and they are good for baking.

Left: Pheasant egg

PHEASANT EGGS

These eggs are of a similar size to those of guinea fowl. They vary in colour from buff to green-blue or olive and can be speckled. They have quite a strong flavour and can be boiled for use in salads, baked or cooked in most other ways. They are available from game dealers and some farm stores. Crack each egg into a cup before adding to other ingredients in case it is bad.

OSTRICH EGGS

Since ostrich meat has grown in popularity, ostrich eggs have become increasingly available. An ostrich egg weighs 450g/1lb or more. It has a comparatively strong flavour and is best used in baking. The pale shells are very thick and hard to crack. Laying is seasonal, during summer and the eggs are usually sold by breeders, delicatessens and specialist stores.

EMU EGGS

The Australian emu is slightly smaller than the ostrich. They are protected in their natural habitat and a special licence is needed for collecting their eggs. However, emus are occasionally farmed for their meat and eggs. They have a winter laying season, during which time one bird will lay about 20 dark blue-green eggs, which have very hard shells. They are best used in baking but they can be scrambled or cooked in savoury dishes.

Above: Pheasant eggs are smaller than hen's eggs and have a much more pronounced flavour.

WILD BIRD EGGS

In most Western countries the eggs of wild birds are protected by legislation preventing their collection as a blanket measure to protect birds whose population is in decline. However, special licences are available for collecting the eggs from gulls, such as the great black-backed gull, the lesser black-backed gull and the herring gull. Gull's eggs are now eaten instead of plover eggs, which used to be considered a great delicacy. Gull's eggs are dark spotted green and brown and they have a mild fishy flavour. On some islands in the North of Scotland, it is possible to obtain a licence to collect gannet and fulmar eggs. Wild bird's eggs are available in season from specialist food stores and game dealers.

Left: An ostrich egg weighs about the same as 9–10 hen's eggs.

Left: An emu egg has an incredibly hard shell.

Buying and Storing Eggs

Many bird's eggs are edible but, in the the kitchen, an egg usually means a hen's egg. There is a wide range of eggs available, such as organic eggs; vegetarian eggs (from hens on a diet free of fishmeal or bonemeal); eggs from hens reared on other types of diet; double-yolked eggs; eggs nutritionally enhanced with omega-3 fatty acids; and even eggs marked as "breakfast eggs" or "weekend eggs". There is also a choice of free-range, barn or cage-produced eggs.

The post-war need to increase food production brought about the change to housing chickens in battery cages. These increased production and helped to control disease, but by the eighties the public became aware of the appalling conditions in which chickens were kept. They were housed high off the ground, in pens from which they could not escape, and with about

14,000 birds to a single hen-house. The realization of the conditions endured by the miserable birds, combined with scares for food safety from increased cases of salmonella, made consumers acutely aware of the cruelty and food safety issues involved.

The image of these birds has put many people off economy eggs and created greater demand for free-range eggs. Some improvements have now been made to the battery system and they are closely monitored and updated throughout the EU. At the same time, doubts have been raised about the hygiene standards of free-range egg production methods.

EGG PRODUCTION METHODS

Hens (pullets) start laying at about 20 weeks old and increase their laying until they lay every day at about 25 weeks old. This continues for 13–15 weeks,

then the laying declines. The average bird now lays about 290 eggs in the first 52 weeks, compared with 123 eggs, which was the average in 1945–6. Eggs are either collected manually and then sorted by eye or, more often, they are collected automatically by conveyor belt leading directly from the laying houses to the packing area.

There is a worldwide dilemma over egg production. The five main egg production methods are free-range, semi-intensive, deep litter, perchery (barn) and caged. In both the EU and the United States of America, legislation has been developed to clarify all methods of egg production. The Farm Animal Welfare Council, the Royal Society for the Prevention of Cruelty to Animals and other animal welfare

Below: Free-range hens are able to wander freely around the farmyard.

groups have developed the Freedom Food approval scheme and such groups continue to strive for the improvement of conditions for egg production all over the world. However, about 80 per cent of all eggs are still produced by the cage system.

Free-range This method allows hens to have continuous access to open-air runs that are mainly covered with vegetation. There may be a maximum of 395 hens per acre of ground, which allows slightly more than 10sq m/ 108sq ft per bird. The buildings must meet certain conditions, such as a constant temperature and a continuous water supply.

Semi-intensive Similar to free-range, this method reduces the space per bird to a minimum of 2.5sq m/9½sq ft.

Deep litter This housed system allows a maximum of 7 hens per sq m/sq yd and at least a third of the floor must be covered with straw or shavings.

Perchery or barn This is a system based on specially designed units with a maximum of 25 birds per sq metre/ sq yd floor space and at least 15cm/ 6in perch space per hen.

Cage This system allows 3–5 hens per cage, with 450sq cm/70sq in per bird with plans to increase the space to 550sq cm/85sq in per bird.

Enriched cages This new scheme will allow 750sq cm/116sq in per bird.

EGG GRADING

Eggs are graded at the packing station, where they are checked for both exterior and interior quality.

In a process known as candling, a light is shone through the eggs so that the contents can be checked without cracking the shell. Modern machinery enables the candler to view the contents of the egg, including the size of the air sac, and automatically remove any eggs with blood spots or imperfections.

If you keep chickens, you can check the internal quality of an egg by holding it up to a candle flame or a bright light in a darkened room. The shell should become sufficiently transparent for you to see if the egg is clear, whether it is fertilized or if there is a blood spot.

Above: During egg candling, an electric light is shone through whole eggs to allow the candler to view their contents.

These blood spots are caused by ruptured blood vessels on the yolk's surface and are not harmful. They are only visible in very fresh eggs and, contrary to popular belief, do not indicate that the egg is fertilized.

Only grade A (EU) or grade A and AA (United States of America) eggs reach the shops. In the USA, the eggs are washed and, as this removes their natural protective bloom, a light tasteless mineral oil is usually applied before packing. Applying an oil is not permitted in the EU. The remaining eggs go to the catering trade; to manufacturing industries for pasteurised egg products; or are used for industrial purposes, not human consumption.

A grade These eggs may be called "Fresh" or, if collected daily, "Extra Fresh". Individual countries have their own national marking and quality guide systems in addition to this EU system. For instance, the Lion Quality is used in the UK and is stamped on the box of 70 per cent of all UK boxed eggs. It indicates that the eggs are fully traceable back to their parent flock, including the feed used. It guarantees that all the pullets in the flock have been vaccinated against salmonella and that the eggs have been transported and stored at temperatures of 20°C/ 68°F or below. These eggs also carry a "best before" date stamp on their shells, which should not exceed 21 days after the egg has been laid.

Loose eggs For those eggs sold unpacked, all information on the producer, quality, weight, best before date and storage advice must be displayed at the point of sale.

Below: Blood spots are caused by ruptured blood vessels. They can look unappetizing but are not harmful.

Left: (left to right) The most commonly available sizes of hen's egg are large, medium and small.

When buying eggs from a farm shop, you may need to look more closely for dirt and cracks. Although controls over eggs sold in farm shops are not as rigid, they should still be refrigerated, or kept at a minimum of 20ºC/68ºF, even if they are very fresh.

Eggs from birds other than chickens, such as bantams, ducks or guinea fowl, are not subject to the same regulations and quality control, so be careful when buying them. The farm should be able to tell when they were collected and, if they have a good turnover, there should be no need for concern.

In the case of wild fowl, such as pheasants, the game keeper may not know when the eggs were laid, so take extra care to ensure that they are still fresh, especially in warmer weather. Crack each egg into a bowl before adding to other ingredients so that any bad ones can be discarded.

Below: Always check boxes of eggs for cracked ones before you buy.

EGG SIZING

The size of an egg can be influenced by a number of factors. The age of a hen is very important, with older hens tending to produce larger eggs. Other contributory factors include breed, weight, diet and stress. Eggs are sized by minimum weight. Small, medium and large are the most common sizes. Size does not make any difference when you are cooking a specific number of eggs, for example when frying, poaching or boiling them. However, when baking, the size of egg can be important because many recipes require accurate proportions of ingredients. Use the chart below to check that you are using the right weight of egg even if you cannot buy the right size.

DATE MARKING

Producers outside USA or EU inspection areas are governed by the laws in their own country or state. In the USA and EU, all boxes of eggs must be date marked. The date of packing, known as the Julian date, is used in the USA. This system gives each day of the year a separate number: day 1 refers to eggs packed on 1st January and day 365 to those packed on 31st December. Boxes may also carry an expiry date after which the eggs cannot be sold. This "best before" date allows for 7 days in a home environment after purchase when the eggs are safe to eat. In addition, the laying date and "sell by" or packing date can be stamped on to the shells in the EU and USA.

CHOOSING EGGS

With all the quality controls that are in operation, there should be little need for thorough checking, but it is always worth looking in the box to make sure that all the eggs are intact and that none are cracked or damaged. You should also check the date stamped on the box or egg, looking for the best before date, sell by date or date of packing. This will help you to work out how fresh the eggs are. Try to buy eggs from a shop that has a fast turnover so that they are really fresh when you buy them. Avoid buying eggs that are already two weeks old unless you know that you will be able to use them within a day or two.

Minimum Weight	EU Classification	USA Classification
73g/2½oz	XL (very large)	Jumbo
63g/2¼oz	L (large)	X Large
53g/2oz	M (medium)	Large
45g/1¾oz	S (Small)	Medium
40g/1½oz		Small
35g/1¼oz		Peewee

STORING FRESH EGGS

Egg shells are porous, making eggs vulnerable to bacteria and odours, which can be absorbed by the egg. To protect them from any smells that can affect their flavour, they should be stored in their box or in a special egg compartment in the fridge, at or below 4°C/40°F. Stored at the right temperature, an egg that is a week old can appear fresher than a day-old egg kept at room temperature. In these conditions eggs can be stored safely for 3–4 weeks. Remove eggs from the fridge a short while before using them for cooking, especially when making meringues, as a better result is often achieved if the eggs are at room temperature.

If you regularly use eggs very quickly and have a suitable cool area, away from sunlight, but well ventilated with fresh air, then the eggs can be stored in wire or wicker baskets or in their box. They will keep for about a week, as long as the temperature is at or below 20°C/68°F and does not fluctuate.

Although eggs should normally be kept away from strong aromas because of their ability to absorb smells, they can be flavoured intentionally. One of

the most well-known methods of flavouring fresh eggs is placing a whole fresh truffle in the egg box for 3–4 days. The delicious, earthy aroma of the truffle will permeate the shell and delicately flavour the egg.

Above: Eggs should be stored unwashed and with the pointed end down to reduce evaporation.

STORING COOKED EGGS

Whole egg should only be stored if fully cooked through. If hard-boiled eggs are left in their shells, they will develop a dark ring around the yolk, which can look unappetizing.

Shelled eggs can be stored in the fridge, loosely wrapped in clear film for 1–2 days, but they will soon acquire a sulphurous smell. If they are to be used in sandwich fillings, for instance, make up the mixture with the freshly cooked egg, then cool and store in the fridge in a well-sealed container or jar.

Omelettes and pancakes, which are intended for use in salads or toppings, can be kept in the fridge for 1–2 days. Chill well, then cover closely in clear film. Do not season the eggs before cooking as they are likely to need more seasoning before serving. Strong flavours, such as onion, garlic, chilli, can affect other foods in the fridge.

Left: Eggs can be stored for a few days in a wicker basket in a cool, well-ventilated room.

STORING LEFTOVERS

When you need only the yolk or the white, the remaining part of the egg can be stored in the fridge for several days until required in another recipe. The yolk can be used to enrich sauces or pastry or make some mayonnaise. Leftover egg white can be used to make a small amount of meringue to top a baked apple or small fruit tarts. Label stored eggs with the quantity and date from the egg box. If you forget to put the number of whites or yolks on the label, remember that an egg weighs about 50g/2oz and the yolk weighs slightly less than half of that. Weigh the yolks or whites to work out how many you have.

To store egg whites, place them in a plastic container or thoroughly cleaned glass jar and cover.

Above: Whole eggs can be stored in an airtight plastic container in the fridge.

Below: Egg whites can be frozen in a small airtight container.

Above: Covering the egg yolk with cold water will prevent it from hardening.

A tough, thick skin forms on whole yolks when they are exposed to air – even the air inside a container is enough to do this. Put the yolks in the smallest container you can find, then pour in enough cold water to cover the yolks and cover the container. To use the yolks, carefully drain off the water.

Beat broken yolks with 15–30ml/ 1–2 tbsp cold water, put into a small container and cover tightly.

FREEZING EGGS

Uncooked eggs that have been removed from their shells can be packed into small sealed containers and frozen. Try to use a container that is just large enough for the egg, so that it contains the minimum of air. Always label containers with the number of eggs and the date. Defrost overnight in the fridge and use as soon as possible.

Above: Protect beaten eggs from drying out by covering with clear film.

How to freeze eggs

1 Lightly beat whole eggs until yolks and whites are blended and pack in small containers.

2 Yolks and whites can be frozen separately in small containers. Yolks thicken on freezing, so beat them lightly, adding either 0.75ml/ ⅛ tsp salt or 7.5ml/1½ tsp sugar to every 4 yolks. Pack in small containers. Label the container, making a note of the date, whether salt or sugar was added and the number of yolks.

3 If you often use eggs in small quantities, or for faster freezing and thawing, pack them in ice-cube trays and cover tightly with clear film. When frozen, transfer the cubes to plastic freezer bags.

4 Cooked whole eggs do not freeze successfully. Hard-boiled egg whites will become tough, rubbery and watery but hard-boiled yolks can freeze well if all the air is excluded.

Above: Lightly beaten whole eggs can be frozen in ice-cube trays.

TESTING FOR FRESHNESS

As soon as the egg is laid, moisture begins to evaporate through the porous shell. Air enters the egg and starts the natural process of deterioration. The warmer the egg, the faster the rate of deterioration. As the egg ages, the membranes that separate the various elements of the egg begin to soften, causing the egg to become flabby.

Above: A very fresh egg has a plump yolk and two distinct layers of white.

Above: A 12-day old egg will have a flatter yolk.

Above: A 21-day old egg will lose the definition between the layers of white.

Above: A fresh egg will sink to the bottom in a glass of water.

Extremely fresh eggs taste delicious and are perfect for poaching, frying and scrambling because they hold together so well. However, if you need to separate whites from yolks, eggs of at least two days old are best. At this stage the whites will not have started to deteriorate but the whites and yolks will not be held together so firmly. As the eggs get older still and the membrane around the yolk deteriorates, you run the risk of breaking the yolk.

Although freshness does not influence the nutritional value of eggs, it does affect their cooking quality. Older eggs spread, looking flatter and flabbier when poached or fried, but they are easier to peel when hard-boiled. For hard-boiled eggs, use eggs that are one to two weeks old because their air sac will have grown larger pushing the egg further from the shell and making it easier to peel.

To check the age of an unlabelled egg, crack the egg on a saucer: a fresh one will have a plump rounded yolk, sitting up well within two distinct layers of white; a 10–12 day old egg will have a far flatter yolk and less definition between the two layers of white; and a 21–28 day old egg will have lost the definition between the separate layers of white, which will have relaxed and blended into each other.

Above: The older the egg, the lighter and more buoyant it is.

It is also possible to check how fresh an egg is without breaking it first. Place the egg in its shell in a glass of cold water. A very fresh egg will contain only a small air sac, so it will be heavier and should lie flat at the bottom of the glass. A very old egg will have a larger air sac, it will weigh less and it will be more buoyant at the blunt end of the egg that contains the air sac. An older egg will settle part way up the water or, if it is extremely old, it will float. If the egg floats it has probably gone bad and should be discarded.

How old is too old?
The recommendation for shops is to only sell eggs that are less than 21 days old. This recommendation is very safe. If eggs are stored under correct conditions, they can be safe for up to 28 days. If you have an egg that may be older than this, you should do one of the above tests before using. However, it is advisable to err on the side of caution and just throw it away. If you are in any doubt, break each egg individually into a cup before mixing it with any other ingredients. The smell will be your final test.

PRESERVED EGGS

Prior to intensive production, hens laid only during warmer weather and eggs had to be stored for the winter. Before freezing and drying were perfected, the most popular method of preserving eggs was in waterglass, a bacteria-resistant solution of sodium silicate, which prevented both the passage of bacteria and the evaporation of the egg content through the porous shell. The eggs were kept in the liquid in a cool place and could be stored for 8–9 months.

Various substances were painted over egg shells in attempts to seal them and prevent deterioration, but the only successful products were oil and Vaseline; both of which are still in controlled use today.

The oldest methods of storing eggs must be those used by Chinese cooks, who have preserved and bottled eggs for centuries. Salted eggs are hard-boiled in their shells and coated in a paste of earth and salt, wrapped in rice husks or grass and tightly packed in a large urn or pan. This is covered tightly and then left in a cold dark place for 30–40 days. These eggs are often used in festive cakes and when they are cut, their bright yellow yolks are revealed. Thousand-year-old eggs are prepared in

a similar way and this also takes about 40 days. They are smothered in a paste of wood ash and lime which turns them a dramatic brown-green colour. The shells need to be soaked before peeling, to allow them to soften. These eggs are eaten with soy sauce and sesame oil. They can also be stir-fried with pork and soy sauce or served as a garnish. If stored untouched, they can last for 2–3 months after preparation.

Left: Thousand-year-old eggs are turned a translucent brown-green colour by the lime and wood ash paste in which they are coated.

EGG PRODUCTS

Various processed forms of egg are available for catering and, to a lesser extent, for use at home. In some countries, such as the UK, where salmonella scares have created demand, pasteurised egg products, using both whole and separated eggs, are available for baking, batters and meringues.

Dried or dehydrated egg was first available during World War II as part of rationing, then it fell out of use until recent years. Dried eggs are now widely used as an ingredient in packet convenience mixes. Dried egg white or whole egg are also available, although less common than specific recipe mixes. Dried whole egg is pasteurised and does not contain added ingredients, so it is ideal for people in weak health who are advised to avoid lightly cooked fresh eggs.

Speciality egg products, which are mainly available to the catering and food service industries, include omelettes, scrambled eggs, French toast, quiches and pancakes.

Modern dried egg products are very easy to use and, compared with the dried egg used in World War II, taste very similar to fresh eggs. Dried egg white, in particular, makes an excellent alternative to fresh, with no difference in taste at all. Dried meringue and royal icing mixes produce admirable results and have the advantage of easy long-term storage. They are ready on the shelf when you need them and are ideal if you only want to use small quantities at a time. Dried whole egg is ideal for scrambling, omelettes, baking and puddings. It is simply blended with the water or added to the other dry ingredients, with the water blended in afterwards.

Above: Thousand-year-old eggs (left) and salted duck eggs take about 40 days to prepare.

The Cooking Properties of Eggs

The physical qualities of egg white and yolk make cooking with eggs complex, fascinating and varied. The different properties of the white and yolk during cooking and preparation produce a diverse range of dishes, from light and airy soufflés and sponges to creamy custards and sauces, crisp batters, and rich mayonnaise.

The features that make eggs such a versatile ingredient are their ability to aerate, coagulate and emulsify or, in simpler terms, their ability to foam, set and thicken.

AERATION

When an egg white is beaten or whisked vigorously, air is trapped within the whites, creating a foam. The slightly gelatinous consistency of egg white makes it ideal for trapping and holding bubbles of air. The more vigorously the whites are beaten, the more air will be trapped, stretching the proteins in the egg white and increasing their bulk six to eight times.

The texture of the foam is affected by the size of the bubbles trapped in the white. Larger bubbles will create a softer, wetter foam, whereas small bubbles create a stiffer, drier foam. The longer the white is whisked, the smaller the bubbles will become. Egg whites become over-whisked when the proteins can stretch no further, creating a very dry, crumbly foam. If you continue to whisk past this point, the whites will eventually break down.

For the best results, egg whites should be brought to room temperature by removing them from the fridge 20–30 minutes before whisking. If an egg is very cold, its white will become more gelatinous, which can affect its ability to incorporate air. Similarly, very young whites have not developed their full elasticity, causing the same problems, while old whites are often too thin and weak to hold the air or their shape. To ensure good results, add a little cream of tartar to egg whites.

Even a little fat will prevent egg whites from whisking to a foam, so it is vital to use a spotlessly clean, grease-free bowl. Egg yolks also contain fat, so it is very important not to drop any into the whites when separating them.

COAGULATION

When an egg is heated, its proteins change from a liquid form to a semi-solid mass, causing the egg to set. This coagulation occurs at a fairly low temperature of 63°C/145°F. This is a vital aspect of successful egg cooking. For example, if meringues are cooked at too high a temperature, they will burn or brown too much before they have fully dried and hardened, whereas if the temperature is too low, the proteins in the egg whites will not set and the sugar will slowly weep out, leaving a sticky mixture on the tray.

Egg yolks contain a higher proportion of protein than egg whites and therefore react even more sensitively to heat.

Because of this, yolks need careful handling when they are cooked to prevent curdling, which occurs when the protein and liquid separate.

To prevent curdling, cornflour can be added to stabilize egg yolk mixtures. This will hold the protein and the liquids together when they are heated and stop them from separating. Many people "cheat" when they make egg custards and pastry sauces by adding cornflour to the mixture. This bypasses the very slow cooking process that would otherwise be necessary.

EMULSION

When a liquid, such as oil, is beaten into an egg, tiny droplets are dispersed evenly throughout the egg, creating a stable mixture. To make a successful emulsion, it is important to use the correct proportion of liquid to egg, otherwise the mixture may not combine properly and is likely to separate. The liquid needs to be beaten into the egg very gradually to allow the egg time to incorporate the liquid. Adding it too quickly is likely to make the mixture separate and curdle.

Classic sauces that rely on the emulsion of egg with another liquid include mayonnaise and hollandaise sauce. Hollandaise sauce relies on heat as well, which melts the butter and allows it to be whisked into the egg. The heat also cooks the yolks very gently, helping the sauce to thicken as the protein in the yolk cooks.

Above: The consistency of egg white is excellent for trapping bubbles of air.

Above: Heat causes the proteins in an egg to solidify.

Above: Oil can be beaten into egg yolk to form an emulsion.

EQUIPMENT

Using the right equipment makes any job easier and usually gives superior results and this is also true for egg cookery. A good whisk will whip up egg whites to new heights and the best pancake pan will allow batter to be set into thin, even crêpes that can be flipped over or tossed with ease.

There is a huge range of cooking utensils available and you may never need most of them, so consider major purchases carefully to make sure they will be useful in your type of cooking: there are lots of small gadgets that are unnecessary for some cooks, but invaluable to others. An egg separator is a good example, as it is a waste of time for experienced chefs who slip yolks from whites in seconds, but very useful for less confident cooks who fret over broken egg shells and traces of yolk in the white.

Baskets

Wire and wicker egg baskets look attractive and stylish in a kitchen and can be used for storing eggs. They should only be used if you are going to use the eggs quickly. Baskets containing eggs should be kept in a cool, airy room or larder at, or below, a temperature of 20°C/68°F. Do not store them in a musty or windowless room.

Above: Wire baskets are often lantern- or hen-shaped.

Left: Wicker baskets are useful for collecting fresh eggs if you keep a few of your own hens.

Below: Egg timers are very useful when cooking eggs.

Timers

A timer is useful for all sorts of cooking, especially when preparing delicate foods such as eggs. A large timer with a rotating dial is good for longer cooking times, but not so accurate for shorter ones. The flat red timer above is specifically designed for eggs: put it in the pan with the eggs and it changes colour, highlighting the words that indicate soft, medium or hard cooking stages. The classic egg timer contains a precise amount of sand or salt sealed into an hourglass-shaped container. The grains takes 3 minutes to pass from the top section to the bottom – the time taken to cook a soft-boiled egg.

Egg piercer

The blunt end of an egg can be pierced before boiling to allow the expanding air in the air sac to escape. Failing to pierce the egg can cause the shell to crack during cooking. An egg piercer is a convenient gadget that pierces the egg simply and efficiently without the risk of breaking the egg. The blunt end of the egg is held gently on the concave surface of the piercer and a pin is pressed through the base of the egg when the button is depressed.

Egg separator

Although eggs can be separated by hand, it takes practice. It is crucial in many recipes, such as meringues, to avoid even the slightest drop of yolk in the whites. A metal egg separator separates the yolk and white easily. The separator is placed on the edge of a small bowl and the whole egg is cracked into it. The yolk drops into the middle of the separator and the white falls through the surrounding slits into the bowl.

Above: Egg separator

Wooden spoons and spatulas

These come in a variety of shapes and those shown here are the most useful for cooking with eggs. The smallest spoon is ideal for making small quantities of egg sauces or scrambled egg, the traditional larger spoon is useful for making sauces and creaming cake mixtures. A spatula with holes is good for beating eggs, while one with slits is ideal for lifting poached and fried eggs from the pan. A large flat spatula will produce chunky scrambled egg and is useful for scraping ingredients from the bottom of a pan.

Egg spoons

These unique implements have three jobs. They can be used to separate the yolk from the white and to beat eggs lightly, and the metal piercer at the end of the handle can be used to pierce the blunt end of eggs before boiling.

Left: A special egg spoon can be used to separate, beat and pierce eggs.

Left: An egg piercer will pierce an egg quickly and easily.

Above: Wooden spoons and spatulas come in all shapes and sizes and are useful for preparing and cooking eggs.

Whisks

There is a selection of sizes and styles of whisk available to suit all tasks.

Wooden and straw whisks can be used to lightly mix ingredients, such as eggs and sauces, but they will not break down lumps or whisk egg whites.

Balloon whisks are shaped like elongated balloons and trap large amounts of air when used properly. The technique is to relax the wrist and rotate the hand. Using the arm can be hard work and does not give the same result. Many experienced cooks and chefs like to roll the balloon whisk back and forth upright between the palms of the hands, working very fast – a method that can be perfected with practice. Although this is ideal when using a small bowl or narrow container, it does not give the maximum volume.

Above from left to right: A small round whisk, a flat whisk, a conical whisk, a long-handled swirled whisk and a rotary whisk are all useful when preparing and cooking eggs.

Small round whisks are useful for mixing small quantities or egg yolks or whites.

Flat whisks give a good airy result when whisking egg whites, but it can take a long time to achieve a very stiff result.

Conical, floppy whisks are useful for sauces and custards.

Long-handled swirled whisks can be used in tall glasses or jugs where there is limited space. They are used in the same way as a balloon whisk.

Rotary whisks, with a pair of beaters, are the best alternative to a hand-held electric beater and are useful for whisking small quantities. They also allow more control than an electric beater.

Right: Balloon whisks come in all sizes, for different tasks, from whisking a spoonful of delicate sauce to whipping up a huge bowl of meringue.

Left: A wooden whisk is best suited to lightly mixing sauces or eggs.

Draining spoons and slices

Large draining spoons and slices are essential for removing eggs from the pan after cooking. Boiled, fried or poached eggs have to be lifted carefully allowing fat or water to drain off before they are transferred to a serving dish. Delicately cooked eggs, such as omelettes, also need to be supported as they are lifted from the pan. Although these tools all perform a similar task, larger rounded spoons are best for fragile poached eggs as they help to keep the egg in a neat shape. Flat, fine-edged slices are better for lifting fried eggs or set omelettes or for cutting them into wedges.

UTENSILS FOR COOKING EGGS

Egg poaching pan

Although this is called a poaching pan, it is actually a steamer. The eggs are cooked in individual cups, in a rack over simmering water. The cups have to be greased and a knob of butter is often used. The result is a cup-shaped egg. The whites can be soft or firm depending on the cooking time; if the water boils too rapidly or for too long, the white can be overcooked and rubbery. One-, two-, and four-egg pans are available.

Above: Draining spoons and slices are good for lifting eggs from a pan.

Egg poaching rings

These rings are designed to keep eggs in a neat shape while they poach. Because the rings prevent the eggs from spreading, it also means that three or four eggs can easily be cooked at the same time.

Above: Poaching rings

Egg coddlers

Traditionally, coddling was a method of gently cooking eggs in water which had been brought to the boil, then set aside to cool. The whole eggs were placed in the water for about 10 minutes, allowing them to set slowly and very softly. Special coddlers are containers into which the eggs can be broken, rather than leaving them in their shells. The coddlers are placed in gently simmering water. The heat must be kept low otherwise the eggs cook too firmly around the outside. Coddlers come in two sizes, one for medium eggs and one for large eggs.

Above: Eggs can be steamed in a poaching pan.

Above: Egg coddlers are used to cook eggs very gently.

Below: Heavy-based omelette pans allow an even spread of heat.

Below: A gently curved non-stick omelette pan helps the omelette to slide easily on to the plate.

Omelette pan

For the best results buy a pan specifically for making omelettes and do not use it for anything else. An omelette pan should be made of aluminium, steel or cast iron and have a thick base throughout which spreads the heat evenly. It should also have gently curving sides so that the omelette slides out easily on to a plate. A steel pan needs to be seasoned by heating it with oil to prevent sticking and should be wiped clean with kitchen paper, not washed with soap and water.

Pancake pan

A pancake pan should be light with low sides that allow the pancake to be tossed easily. Steel is often used for these pans, but there are also good lightweight non-stick pancake pans. A steel pan needs seasoning and wiping clean to prevent the pancakes from sticking. To season, slowly heat a little oil in the pan until it begins to smoke. Rub the inside of the pan with kitchen paper, then rinse and dry thoroughly.

Above and left: Pancake pans help to produce thin, even pancakes.

Gratin dishes

These shallow ovenproof dishes, available in various sizes, are ideal for baked eggs with cream and added ingredients, such as vegetables or spiced sausages. They are also used to hold gratinéed fruits or other foods topped with a sabayon sauce, which are then browned in the oven or under the grill.

Ramekins

These are like miniature soufflé dishes and are usually straight-sided and deep. Ramekins are used for individual portions, such as savoury or sweet mousses, baked eggs and custards. The food may be served in the dish or the dish can act as a mould from which the food is turned out for serving. When cooking delicate dishes, such as custards, ramekins are usually placed in a *bain-marie*, a roasting tin (pan) into which water is poured; this protects the mixture from overcooking round the sides of the dish.

Ramekins allow food to cook evenly and their undersides are unglazed, so that the heat penetrates the dish quickly. They are available in white porcelain, ovenproof glass, pottery and many modern china designs that match tableware. The thicker the ramekin, the slower the cooking. Remember that thick ramekins retain heat and food will carry on cooking for some time after it is removed from the oven.

OVENPROOF DISHES

Soufflé dishes

A soufflé dish is characterized by its straight sides. This helps a hot soufflé mixture to rise high and straight. It is often better to use a dish that is slightly too small as this will make the soufflé rise higher. These dishes are also used for chilled soufflés. A paper collar can be tied around the dish to support the mixture while it sets. When the collar is removed, the soufflé will stand above the top of the dish. White porcelain dishes are the classic choice.

Above: Gratin dishes are ideal for baking eggs in the oven.

Below: Soufflé dishes are available in a range of sizes, from small individual ones to very large dishes for several people.

Below: Plain white porcelain ramekins are available in a variety of sizes.

Food processors

The food processor has revolutionized food preparation. This fast appliance makes light work of mayonnaise, batters, sauces, pastries and certain cake mixtures. Although small quantities can be processed, many food processors are designed to hold larger quantities and these do not process small quantities efficiently. For example, a small amount of mayonnaise is likely to be lost on the side of the bowl. Select a processor with a slow speed or pulse setting for precise control when preparing delicate mixtures, such as hollandaise sauce. Be careful not to over-process foods.

Above:
A blender is
great for making
pancake batters.

Above: An electric omelette maker will cook delicious omelettes in minutes.

ELECTRICAL APPLIANCES

Blenders

If you enjoy making mayonnaise and pancakes, you will find a blender invaluable.
Single unit blenders, with a jug on top of the machine, are quick and easy to use and the jug can be immersed in water or taken apart for washing.
Hand blenders, with a purpose-built jug, work quickly and easily, but they do not process larger quantities or tough ingredients.
Free-standing electric mixers, with balloon whisk, beater and extra large bowl are good for making cakes or meringues. A stainless steel bowl is an optional extra. These large food mixers are slower than a food processor, so they can be left to whisk, beat or mix while you work on another part of the recipe. Larger mixers come with a range of optional attachments, including a blender.

Electric omelette makers

An electric omelette maker can cook two small omelettes in a couple of minutes. The heated cooking hollows are brushed with oil or butter to help browning. Any filling is cooked first, then the beaten egg mixture is poured into the hollow, and the lid closed to cook the omelette.

Left: A large, free-standing mixer has a range of useful attachments.

MICROWAVE EGG GADGETS

For those who enjoy microwave cooking, there are several gadgets available that are specifically designed for cooking eggs. The gadgets are essential for some techniques, such as boiling. It is not possible to boil an egg in a microwave as the unpunctured shell is likely to burst. A special microwave egg boiler has hollows for holding the eggs and a lid. The pot of eggs is placed inside the lidded container, with a little water in the base. This allows the eggs to be cooked safely, without the fear of them bursting.

UTENSILS FOR SERVING EGGS

As well as specialist equipment for cooking, there are also a number of utensils that can be useful for serving cooked eggs.

Above, clockwise from top right: Special microwave gadgets include an omelette dish, egg coddlers, four- and two-egg poaching dishes and a boiling dish.

Egg slicer

Eggs can be difficult to slice neatly. If you make lots of egg sandwiches, or want neat slices as a garnish, a slicer is invaluable. The cold hard-boiled egg is placed in the hollow and then the frame of wires is gently pulled down to cut the egg into neat slices.

Above: An egg cutter will cut the top off a boiled egg neatly and cleanly.

Egg cutters

These round-bladed, deeply serrated scissors are designed for cutting the tops off boiled eggs or at least cracking the top of the shell, ready for a spoon to be used to slip off the top of the egg.

Egg cups

These are essential for holding the awkward-shaped boiled egg steady so that it can be opened and eaten with a spoon. Choice is personal, depending on design and colour. Some egg cups have lids to keep the eggs hot until they are taken to the table.

Left: Egg cups are ideal for holding hot boiled eggs steady and are available in a variety of shapes and sizes.

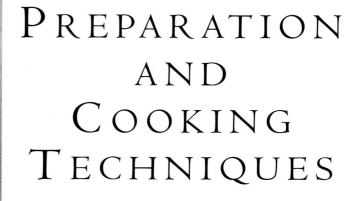

PREPARATION AND COOKING TECHNIQUES

The joy of cooking with eggs lies both in their simplicity and their versatility. This chapter guides you through all the key techniques that are essential for the successful preparation and cooking of eggs. From the most basic boiling to more complicated advice on making soufflés, roulades and meringues, the range of techniques proves the true versatility of the egg as a cooking ingredient.

BASIC COOKING TECHNIQUES

Eggs are easy to cook and incredibly versatile, adapting well to a wide variety of cooking techniques. Understanding what happens to an egg when it is heated and cooked helps to make sense of cooking techniques and methods using eggs. Made up of white (albumen) and yolk, an egg consists of mainly water, fat and protein, with smaller proportions of other elements and nutrients. The white is mainly water with protein; the yolk contains fat, protein and other nutrients.

In terms of basic cooking techniques, the protein in egg makes the most impact: when heated it becomes firm. The longer it is heated, or the hotter the temperature, the firmer it becomes. If an egg is heated too fiercely or for too long, the protein sets too firmly for good eating, which is why overcooked eggs become tough.

When beaten, the proteins from the white combine with those in the yolk and will set at a slightly higher temperature. Instead of the firm white and soft yolk of boiled or fried eggs, beaten eggs can be cooked gently until creamy in texture, as when scrambled or made into an omelette. Cooked over too high a heat, or for too long, scrambled eggs curdle when the protein sets hard and separates leaving a watery residue.

Controlling the heat and length of cooking is the key to cooking eggs successfully. Generally, when making plain cooked eggs, the temperature should not be too high: "very hot" is "too hot". There are exceptions, for example when frying eggs or making an omelette, but in both these cases the high temperature is balanced by very brief cooking, ensuring that the egg does not have time to become tough.

SEPARATING EGGS

When cracking eggs, especially if you intend separating the yolk from the white, make a neat crack around the middle of the shell. Have two bowls ready and, as soon as the shell is cracked, lift the egg, holding both halves together, to stop the yolk from falling into the bowl.

1 To crack the egg, using a single, sharp movement, tap the egg firmly on the side of the bowl as near to the middle of the shell as possible. Alternatively, make an indent in the shell by tapping the egg with the blade of a knife.

2 Use your thumbs to prise the shell halves apart gently, trying to break the shell as little as you possibly can. Turn the shell half containing the yolk upright and let the white from both halves drop into the bowl below.

3 Tilt the shell halves to slip the yolk from one to the other, being careful not to break the yolk. Let the excess white fall into the bowl. Repeat until most of the white has been transferred to the bowl. Slip the yolk into the second bowl and check that there is no more white left in either of the shells.

PIERCING EGGS

Very fresh or cold eggs may crack when placed in boiling water. Although it does not affect the flavour or texture of the egg, it can leave unattractive lumps of cooked white on the outside of the shell. To help prevent the shell from cracking during cooking, pierce the rounded end of the egg, which contains an air space. This allows the expanding air to escape without cracking the shell.

Use a pin to make a small hole in the shell. Pierce the shell gently, by rotating the pin to "drill" a hole. Do not press too hard as this could crack the shell.

Alternatively, use a specially designed egg piercer to make a hole in the shell. Once pierced, immerse the egg in hot water and bring back to the boil.

BOILING EGGS

Eggs should never be boiled rapidly as this is too fast and fierce, frequently causing the shells to crack and resulting in whites with a very rubbery texture. Although eggs can be added to cold water, timing is more accurate when they are added to water that is simmering steadily or boiling gently. Start timing the cooking when the water is bubbling gently again. When preparing soft-boiled eggs for further cooking with other ingredients, cook them for fractionally less time than recommended, then plunge them straight into cold water. When cooking hard-boiled eggs for salads and garnishes, turn or stir the eggs gently once or twice in the first minute of cooking so that the yolks stay in the middle, then they will look neat when sliced or cut. Freshly laid eggs should be kept for 2–3 days if they are to be hard boiled, otherwise they are difficult to shell.

Simmering and Boiling Eggs

Water simmers when it is on the verge of boiling. Usually, it is brought to the boil first, then the heat is reduced and regulated to keep the water moving gently, with the occasional bubble breaking the surface. When the water only just moves, it is simmering gently; when bubbles regularly break the surface, it is simmering steadily. It is possible to boil water gently, so that bubbles break the surface lightly, instead of boiling rapidly and constantly, when bubbles break rapidly and constantly.

Making Perfect Boiled Eggs

1 When cooking chilled eggs until firm, it is best to put them into cold water.

2 Alternatively, lower the eggs on a spoon into simmering water, taking care not to let them drop on to the base of the pan or they will crack.

3 Heat the water until bubbling gently, then begin timing the cooking, using the table below.

Cooking times

This is a guide to cooking eggs added to hot water. Start timing the cooking when the water boils gently. The timings for cooking eggs that are added to cold water are very similar to those for hot water. Reduce cooking time by about 30 seconds. Cooking times can vary significantly if the eggs are very cold, very fresh or very old. Allow an extra 30 seconds for really fresh eggs (less than 48 hours old) and more if they are very cold.

	Cooking time in minutes		
	Small	Medium	Large
Soft	3	4	4½–5
Semi-firm	4	5–6	6–7
(yolks still soft)			
Hard	7	8–10	10–12

SHELLING AND SERVING BOILED EGGS

Soft-boiled eggs should be eaten immediately. If they have to stand for 1–2 minutes, crack their tops lightly with the back of spoon or an egg cutter to allow steam to escape and prevent the eggs from cooking further. If they are to be used in other dishes, they should be peeled as soon as they are cool enough to handle.

Eggs are easier to shell when completely cold, so plunge them into cold water immediately after cooking and change the water several times to keep it cold. To prevent black rings from forming around the egg yolks, crack the shells all over with the back of a spoon as soon as the eggs are cooked, and cool the eggs as quickly as possible by placing them in a bowl of cold water. If shelled eggs are not used immediately, store them in cold water in the fridge.

How to Serve a Boiled Egg

Use an egg cutter to make a slight crack all around the shell so that the top can be removed easily with a spoon.

Alternatively, cut off the top with a small sharp knife. Tap the shell firmly and evenly with the blade to prevent too much shell from crumbling.

How to Shell a Boiled Egg

1 As soon as the egg is boiled, remove it from the pan and place in a bowl of very cold water. When it has cooled enough to handle, crack the egg shell evenly all over with a teaspoon or tap it gently on a work surface.

2 Start peeling off the shell at the rounded end, where there should be a gap under the shell from the air sac. Lift off the shell and its underlying membrane together, then the shell will peel off easily in large segments. If the shell does not come away from the egg easily, hold it under cold running water for a few seconds.

Eggs for garnishing

Hard-boiled egg can be used for a wide variety of garnishes. The eggs should look attractive and appetizing, so take care to cook them perfectly, crack them immediately and cool them quickly. Make sure that they cool completely before cutting.

Using an egg slicer

To cut thin, even slices, use an egg slicer. For the best results use cold, hard-boiled eggs and lightly oil the wires so that they slip through the egg white without breaking it.

Chopping hard-boiled eggs

Use a large knife with a lightly oiled blade to halve or quarter the egg, then chop coarsely or finely, as required. Finely chopped hard-boiled egg can be used to garnish salads or dishes such as savoury mousses or foods set in aspic. Chopped egg can also be used on open sandwiches.

Sieving hard-boiled eggs

Press the yolk and white separately through a fine sieve and use one or both to garnish cold poached fish, dressed crab, savoury mousses and cold soups. Sieved egg can also be used to garnish egg mayonnaise or stuffed eggs.

1 Cooked egg yolk is very soft and is therefore easy to press through a fine sieve, and can be sieved on to a board, directly into salads, or over vegetables or soups.

2 Cooked egg white has a slightly firmer consistency than yolk and will need to be pressed through the sieve quite hard, using the back of a spoon. It is usually easier to press the egg white through the sieve on to a board or into a bowl, rather than directly on to the dish to be garnished. The sieved egg white can then be sprinkled on to the dish.

Stuffing eggs

Hard-boiled eggs can be stuffed with many different fillings. Use a teaspoon to scoop out the yolks from halved hard-boiled eggs, then mash them with the chosen filling ingredients. These eggs are perfect for parties because they can be prepared in advance, then chilled until required.

1 Soft-textured fillings, such as a herb and garlic mixture, cream cheese or flavoured mayonnaise can be spooned into the hollows in the whites using two teaspoons.

2 Smooth but firm mixtures, such as this paste made from the egg yolk, tomato, chilli and anchovy essence, can be piped back into the egg whites from a piping bag fitted with a fairly large nozzle. Use a swirling motion to give an attractive finish.

POACHING EGGS

This simple cooking method still provokes debate about whether to add salt or vinegar, make the water swirl, causing the egg white to wrap itself around the yolk, or add the egg and turn off the heat. All are successful in their own way, but adding salt does encourage the egg to spread. It is important to use really fresh eggs, otherwise the whites spread into wisps.

A poaching ring can be used to help keep the egg in shape. A poaching pan can also be used but this gives a slightly different result: the whites tend to be firmer and the egg is saucer-shaped and similar to a soft-boiled egg.

Making Classic Poached Eggs

1 Pour about 2.5–4cm/1–1½in water into a frying pan. Add 15ml/1 tbsp vinegar and bring to the boil. Reduce the heat, if necessary, to keep the water bubbling gently. Crack the egg into a cup or small dish so that you can control its position easily when adding it to the pan, then gently tip it into the bubbling water.

2 Cook the egg very gently for 1 minute undisturbed. Then gently spoon a little water over the centre of the egg to cook the yolk.

3 The egg is cooked when it can be loosened easily from the bottom of the pan. Use a skimmer, draining spoon or fish slice to lift the egg from the water.

4 Trim off any rough edges, using a pair of kitchen scissors. Allow any water to run off the egg and pat dry with kitchen paper before transferring it to a plate or serving dish.

Using a Poaching Ring

To use a poaching ring, place a lightly oiled ring in a pan of gently bubbling water and tip an egg into the ring from a cup. Cook for 1 minute until the white begins to set round the edge. Spoon over boiling water and cook for a further 1–2 minutes, until the top is set. Run a knife around the inside of the ring, lift the egg and ring out of the pan and remove the ring. Drain and serve.

Steam-poaching Eggs

Eggs can be steamed in a poaching pan. A tray of poaching cups holds the eggs out of the simmering water. Partly fill the pan with water and bring to a gentle boil. Add a knob of butter to each of the individual cups and, when the butter has melted, tip an egg into each one. Cover the pan with a lid and cook for 3 minutes until the top of the egg is just firm. To serve, loosen the egg gently with a round-ended knife and slide on to hot buttered toast.

CODDLING EGGS

This is a very gentle cooking method, giving delicate results. Add the eggs to the pan as for boiling and bring the water to a gentle boil, then cover the pan and remove it from the heat. Leave the eggs to stand for 5–6 minutes for a soft-boiled egg or 7–8 minutes for a firmer set. This cooks the eggs evenly.

Using an Egg Coddler

To use an egg coddler, butter the dish and crack an egg into it. Sprinkle with salt and pepper, replace the lid and place in a pan to simmer for 6–10 minutes, depending on the size of egg used. For a very soft result, turn off the heat and leave to stand for several minutes. Serve the egg in the dish.

BAKING EGGS

Oven-baked eggs in ramekins are delicate, and quick and easy to prepare. They can be flavoured or enriched with a variety of ingredients, such as cream, garlic, ham or cheese, to make delicious starters or light meals. Cover the eggs with foil to prevent the yolks from overcooking.

1 Preheat the oven to 180°C/350°F/Gas 4. Lightly butter the ramekins and crack an egg into each. Top with a knob of butter and a little seasoning.

2 Stand the ramekins in a roasting tin (pan), half filled with hot water. Bake for 15–18 minutes, until the whites are set.

SCRAMBLING EGGS

These were originally called buttered eggs. Beaten eggs are gently stirred in hot butter over heat until they set. They can be soft and creamy or cooked until quite firm and dry. Water or milk can also be added.

Ingredients can be added to turn plain scrambled eggs into a variety of quick light supper dishes or sandwich fillings. Chopped fresh ingredients such as herbs, diced cooked ham, chopped tomatoes, sliced mushrooms and crushed garlic all go well with scrambled eggs. Store-cupboard ingredients, such as anchovy fillets, tuna, frozen peas or canned beans, can also be used.

Scrambled eggs are usually served on toast, but there are many other ways to serve them. Try them on toasted muffins, crumpets or pitta bread. Serve scrambled eggs in baked potatoes or with small pasta shapes, or add them to a bed of cooked spinach.

Making Scrambled Eggs

1 Lightly beat the eggs with seasoning to taste. Allow 3 eggs per person. Heat about 15g/½oz/1 tbsp butter in a small saucepan until sizzling. Quickly pour in the eggs and stir.

2 Stir the egg mixture frequently over a medium heat for 1–2 minutes, until the eggs are lightly set but still very moist and creamy.

3 For more firmly set scrambled egg, with a slightly drier texture, do not stir quite so frequently and cook for about 4 minutes.

4 If you prefer scrambled eggs with a chunkier texture, use a flat-ended wooden spoon or spatula and stir only occasionally, turning over larger flakes of egg every time.

FRYING EGGS

Eggs can be shallow fried or deep fried. Shallow frying with little or no oil is the healthier method, but when deep fried briefly and well drained, eggs are wonderfully crisp. For both methods the eggs should be very fresh. Fresh light vegetable oil is usually used but a knob of butter can be added when shallow frying. The fat must be hot enough for the eggs to bubble and cook as soon as they are added to the pan, but not so hot that they break up.

Shallow Frying Eggs

1 Heat 30–45ml/2–3 tbsp oil in a heavy-based frying pan over a medium heat. There is no need to add oil to a non-stick pan. Crack the egg into the pan and allow it to settle and start bubbling gently around the edges before basting or adding another egg.

2 After 1 minute, spoon a little hot oil over the yolk to cook the egg evenly.

3 Cook for a further 1 minute, until the white has become completely opaque and the edges are just turning brown. If you prefer a firmer yolk, cook the egg for a further minute. Use a fish slice to lift the egg out of the pan, carefully allowing oil to drain off for a few seconds or, alternatively, place briefly on a piece of kitchen paper.

4 Alternatively, if you prefer a firmer, crisper egg still, gently flip the egg over, using a fish slice, and cook for a further minute.

Fried eggs in butter sauce

1 Melt 15ml/1 tbsp butter until it begins to foam. Break an egg into the hot butter and cook for about 1 minute until it begins to set.

2 Carefully turn the egg over using a spatula or fish slice that will support the yolk and as much of the white as possible.

3 Cook for a few more seconds until the white around the yolk has set, then remove from the heat. Slide the egg onto a warmed plate to keep warm.

4 To make the sauce, return the pan to the heat and melt about 15ml/1 tbsp butter until it foams. Add a dash of balsamic vinegar and cook for a few more seconds. Pour over the egg and serve.

Deep Frying Eggs

1 Crack the egg into a cup or small bowl so that you can slip it quickly and easily into the pan without splashing yourself with hot oil.

2 Heat about 2.5cm/1in vegetable or sunflower oil in a deep frying pan to 180°C/350°F or until it is hot enough to turn a cube of day-old bread brown in about 45 seconds. Gently tip the egg into the hot oil.

3 Cook the egg for 30 seconds, then use a draining spoon to turn or fold it over carefully.

4 Cook for a further 30 seconds or until the egg white is crisp and golden on both sides. Use the draining spoon to remove the egg and drain it on kitchen paper before serving.

BASIC METHODS AND MIXTURES

The magic of cooking with eggs unfolds when they are combined with other ingredients in simple mixtures. These basic methods and mixtures form the basis for the incredible array of dishes that rely on eggs for their success.

Beating and whisking changes the way eggs behave during cooking. Simply beating the white with the yolk creates a mixture that looks quite different from a basic egg; add sugar to this and the mixture will become thick, light and creamy on further beating. When an egg white is whisked it traps a large amount of air, becomes foamy and will stand up in peaks. Being able to trap air in eggs and egg mixtures gives the cook access to a range of methods for both savoury and sweet dishes that will achieve wonderfully varied results.

When mixtures containing eggs are heated, the basic principle of setting, or the protein becoming firm, is true. However, when eggs are combined with air and other ingredients their taste and texture can be very different from that of a whole cooked egg. The following methods and mixtures show how eggs can act as raising agents and lighten other ingredients to set.

BATTERS

A batter is usually a mixture made of flour and a liquid such as milk. Egg is added to the majority of batters. Mixed to different consistencies, a basic flour, egg and milk batter can be used to make any number of wonderful dishes: thin French crêpes, large pancakes or small, thick drop scones (Scotch pancakes or breakfast pancakes in America) and baked specialities, such as Yorkshire pudding and a French batter pudding called *clafoutis*. With additional raising agents, batters are used for waffles, crumpets and blinis (yeasted buckwheat pancakes). Batters for some dishes, such as pancakes, are allowed to rest after mixing so that the air bubbles subside. When a batter is left to rest, it should be kept cold and covered. If there is any delay before cooking the batter, or you have any left over, it should be chilled.

Making Batter

1 Beat 2 eggs well with an electric beater or by hand.

2 Start to beat in 125g/4oz/1 cup flour until the mixture is too thick to continue. There is no need to sift the flour as any lumps will be beaten out.

3 Add a little milk and the remaining flour and beat to a paste. Gradually add 250ml/8fl oz/1 cup milk and beat until smooth. Set aside for 20 minutes.

4 To make the batter in a blender or food processor, process the flour, egg and a little milk to a paste, then add the remaining milk and process until smooth.

Variations on Basic Batter

Batter can be made with other liquids, such as water, stock or wine. Fizzy beer or cider can be used to lighten batters.

Batter can be flavoured with 15–30ml/ 1–2 tbsp chopped herbs, garlic, mustard, grated citrus rind or a little sugar.

Making Little Yorkshire Puddings

1 Preheat the oven to 220°C/425°F/ Gas 7 for large puddings or 230°C/ 450°F/Gas 8 for small puddings.

2 Place a little fat in the tin (pan). Heat in the oven for 3–5 minutes until very hot.

3 Pour in the batter – the fat should sizzle at once. Bake for 25–30 minutes, reducing the heat to 180°C/350°F/ Gas 4 halfway through cooking time for smaller items.

Making Pancakes

Pancakes are cooked individually, so layer them between sheets of kitchen paper and keep warm in the oven while you cook the remaining batter.

1 Heat a little oil in a pancake pan or frying pan. Pour in a little batter, made with an extra egg. As you do so, tilt and swirl the pan to coat the bottom with a thin, even layer of batter.

2 Cook over a medium heat until golden underneath. To toss, loosen the edges then slide the pancake to the pan's rim.

3 Jerk the pan upwards, then hold it in the same place to catch the pancake. Alternatively, turn it with a palette knife.

4 Cook until the second side is golden, then slide out on to kitchen paper.

Drop Scones

MAKES 18

INGREDIENTS
  225g/8oz/2 cups self-raising
    flour (self-rising flour)
  2.5ml/½ tsp salt
  15ml/1 tbsp caster
    (superfine) sugar
  1 egg, beaten
  300ml/½ pint/1¼ cups milk
  oil, for cooking

1 Preheat a griddle or heavy-based frying pan. Sift the flour and salt into a bowl and stir in the sugar. Make a well in the centre.

2 Add the egg and half the milk, then gradually incorporate the flour to make a smooth paste. Gradually beat in the remaining milk until smooth.

3 Lightly oil the griddle or frying pan. Drop tablespoons of batter on to the surface, leaving them until they bubble and the bubbles begin to burst.

4 Turn the drop scones over and cook them until the undersides are golden. Keep the cooked drop scones warm and moist by wrapping them in a clean napkin while cooking successive batches.

OMELETTES

Lightly beaten eggs, seasoned and fried to form a light omelette provides a meal in about 3 minutes. Any number of seasonings, fillings or toppings can be added to make an omelette more substantial. Thick, set omelettes can be served cold, cut into small portions to make finger food. When the whites are whisked and folded into the yolks, a plain omelette is elevated to soufflé omelette status. With a rich fruit filling, soufflé omelettes make luxurious, yet light desserts.

Although special omelette pans are available, any heavy based, medium non-stick frying pan will do. Prepare the flavourings and fillings first. Have a warmed serving plate ready and do not cook the omelette until you are ready to eat it. Traditionally rolled or folded to enclose a filling, an omelette can also be served flat and topped with any flavouring ingredients.

Making a Classic Omelette

1 Allow 3 eggs per omelette. Lightly beat the eggs with seasonings.

2 Heat 15g/½ oz/1 tbsp butter in an omelette or frying pan until very hot and sizzling, but not smoking or browning. Pour in the eggs, tilting the pan slightly.

3 Cook the eggs for a few seconds until the base has set, then use a fork to push in the sides or stir gently. The idea is to ensure that the unset egg mixture runs on to the hot pan and starts cooking. Cook for about 1 minute or until the egg is just beginning to set. For a firmer set, cook for a little longer.

4 Use a large flat spatula to fold over a third of the omelette.

5 Tilting the pan away from you, flip the omelette over again and slide it out immediately on to a warmed serving plate in one action.

COOK'S TIP
For the perfect omelette, the egg in the middle should still be slightly runny or creamy when served, but the omelette can be completely set if preferred.

Making a Soufflé Omelette

The eggs are separated and the whites whisked until stiff. The whites are then folded into the yolk mixture to give a large volume of light mixture. A savoury or sweet filling may be added to the cooked omelette, which must be served promptly before it collapses.

1 Separate the eggs. Beat the yolks with seasoning or a little sugar in a large bowl. Whisk the whites until stiff, then fold them into the yolks. Preheat the grill (broiler) on the hottest setting.

2 Heat 15g/½oz/1 tbsp butter in an omelette pan or frying pan and spoon in the mixture, spreading it out evenly.

3 Cook gently for 2–3 minutes, until the mixture is golden and firm underneath and only just firm on top.

4 The omelette can be served as it is or finished under the grill. Hold the pan under the grill for a few seconds, keeping it slightly away from the heat as the omelette will rise. Cook for a few seconds until lightly browned on top.

5 Spoon the chosen filling or fruit conserve over a third of the omelette.

6 Use a large spatula to fold the cooked omelette in half and immediately transfer it to a warm serving plate.

To add the professional-looking skewer marks on top, heat a greased skewer in a gas flame until almost glowing. Then press the skewer gently, but firmly, on the top of the omelette to mark diagonal lines. A sweet omelette can be dredged with icing (confectioners') sugar before being scored in this way.

SET THICK OMELETTES

Instead of folding or topping a lightly cooked thin omelette to incorporate a filling, the ingredients can be set in the beaten egg mixture. For a set thick omelette, a much larger proportion of flavouring ingredients are used, usually vegetables such as potato and onion. The mixture is cooked very slowly until set. The cooked omelette can be served hot, warm or cold, cut into wedges or fingers. Spanish tortilla and Italian frittata are both set omelettes.

Making Spanish Omelette

1 Heat a mixture of butter and oil in a large heavy-based pan, then add sliced potatoes and onions and cook gently until almost tender. Beat 6 eggs with seasoning, a crushed garlic clove and plenty of chopped parsley. Pour the eggs evenly over the hot vegetables. Continue cooking gently for 4–5 minutes or until the egg has almost set.

2 Place a plate over the top of the pan. Put your hand firmly on the top and hold the pan with a cloth, then quickly turn over both pan and plate together.

3 Lift off the pan and allow the omelette to slip out on to the plate.

4 Slide the omelette back into the pan, cooked side up, and continue cooking until set and golden underneath. Serve hot or cool, cut into slices or wedges, with salad as an accompaniment.

Omelette fillings
For a thin folded omelette, try sliced mushrooms, sautéed in a little butter; a sprinkling of grated cheese, such as Cheddar, with chopped parsley; or 1–2 spoonfuls of chopped smoky ham.

Sweet soufflé omelettes are best served with a fruit filling such as a really good conserve, warmed with a splash or two of brandy to help it spread, or try fresh raspberries, flamed in liqueur, with cream.

For a thick set omelette, try adding lightly sautéed spinach or courgette (zucchini), or slices of spicy sausage to the basic potato and onion filling.

USING EGGS FOR BINDING, COATING AND GLAZING

Eggs are perfect for these three tasks. They bind ingredients in burgers, pâtés and similar dishes, ensuring they retain their shape during cooking. Together with flour and breadcrumbs, eggs make a delicate coating for fine foods. They are also used to lighten batters that coat and protect foods during frying. Beaten egg or egg yolk give an attractive golden glaze to many baked items.

Binding with Egg

Eggs can be added to the ingredients for burgers, pâtés, fish cakes, potato cakes, rissoles, meatloaves and similar mixtures. As the mixture cooks, the egg sets and helps to hold the ingredients together. Add 1 egg to every 450g/1lb ingredients.

Simple fish cakes
In a large bowl, mix together 200g/7oz can tuna or salmon with 300g/11oz/2¾ cups mashed potatoes. Season with 30ml/2tbsp chopped fresh parsley or dill, salt and freshly ground black pepper, then mix in 1 beaten egg. Shape the mixture into eight patties. Dip each pattie in beaten egg, then coat in fine white breadcrumbs.
Grill (broil) the fishcakes on both sides until golden brown and crisp. Serve the fishcakes hot with grilled tomatoes or steamed courgettes (zucchini).

Coating with Egg and Breadcrumbs

Coating food, such as rissoles, potato cakes and fish and shellfish, with egg and breadcrumbs protects it from fierce heat during frying. Cover the food in flour, then dip in beaten egg and finally coat in fine white breadcrumbs. When cooked, the coating is deliciously crisp and golden and the filling is very moist.

Glazing with Egg

Pastries and breads, particularly savoury items, bake to a rich golden finish when brushed lightly with beaten egg. Whole beaten egg may be used or, for a very rich glossy finish, egg yolk can be lightly beaten with a little water and a pinch of salt or sugar. Beaten egg can also be used to seal the surface of pastry. Brush egg white over the base of a pastry case to prevent the filling from oozing into the pastry or brush beaten whole egg on pastry edges that need to be sealed together, such as the top and bottom of a pie crust.

SAVOURY EGG SAUCES

Many classic savoury sauces are based on egg, either emulsified with hot butter or a good oil, or cooked slowly with a little liquid and whisked continuously over a gentle heat. The results are wonderfully luscious. Soft, velvet-textured egg and butter hollandaise sauce complements simple grilled (brifish or vegetables, while Béarnaise sauce is perfect for grilled meats, especially steak.
    Patience and a gentle touch are vital when making sauces. Fierce heat and fast cooking or mixing can ruin egg-based mixtures. For the more cautious, cook butter sauces very slowly in a bowl placed over a saucepan of simmering water – be warned, this does take a very long time. When you are more confident sauces can be made in a small heavy-based saucepan over gentle heat.

Making Hollandaise Sauce

1 Whisk 3 large egg yolks in a saucepan with a few drops of white wine vinegar, 15ml/1 tbsp lemon juice and seasoning.

2 Heat 175g/6oz/¾ cup butter until bubbling. Gradually pour into the egg mixture, whisking continuously over a very gentle heat. Cook slowly, whisking more frequently as the sauce heats. Whisk very fast if any lumps appear.

3 Continue cooking very slowly, stirring or whisking continuously, until the sauce is thick and velvety. Use immediately or keep warm.

4 If the sauce begins to curdle, remove from the heat and transfer to a bowl, then whisk until the sauce cools.

Making Béarnaise Sauce

1 Boil 2 chopped shallots, 1 sliced garlic clove, 4 black peppercorns and a few sprigs of fresh parsley and tarragon in 30ml/2 tbsp water and 60ml/4 tbsp wine vinegar until reduced by half. Meanwhile, beat 3 large egg yolks and melt 175g/6oz/¾ cup butter until hot.

2 Strain the hot vinegar and pour on to the egg yolks, whisking continuously. Then whisk in the hot butter and follow steps 2, 3 and 4 for hollandaise sauce.

Keeping butter sauces warm

These hot sauces can be made in advance and kept warm. Cover with clear film and press it on the surface to prevent any air from entering. Place the bowl over a pan of warm water. Alternatively, if the sauce has been covered and left to go cold, it can be reheated gently in the microwave.
   Butter sauces can be made a day ahead and chilled or they can even be frozen. Reheat gently, whisking all the time before serving.

MAYONNAISE

Unlike cooked butter sauces, creamy mayonnaise achieves its thick and glossy texture by beating alone. A mild-flavoured oil is gradually beaten into an egg to create a thick emulsion.

Making Mayonnaise

1 Whisk 1 large egg in a mixing bowl with seasoning, 2.5ml/½ tsp French mustard and the juice of ½ small lemon or 30ml/2 tbsp white wine vinegar.

2 Prepare 600ml/1 pint/2½ cups oil: a mixture of good vegetable oil or sunflower oil and light olive oil mixed half and half is suitable.

3 Whisking continuously, slowly pour in the oil in a very fine stream. For a richer mayonnaise, use 2 egg yolks and allow about 300ml/½ pint/1¼ cups olive oil.

4 Keep whisking and adding oil, until the mixture thickens to form a smooth, glossy mayonnaise. A large egg should take most of the oil. Chill until required.

5 Mayonnaise can be stored in the fridge in an airtight jar for about a week.

Making mayonnaise in a food processor or blender
As with butter sauces, time and patience are vital to a successful mayonnaise. However, it can be made quickly and easily in a food processor or blender. Care still needs to be taken when adding the oil because adding it too quickly can cause mayonnaise to separate.
   It is best to make larger quantities as small amounts of mayonnaise are lost against the sides of the bowl or jug. Blend together the egg and flavourings. With the machine running, gradually drizzle in the oil, a little at a time, until the mixture thickens to form a glossy mayonnaise.

Soufflé effects

Give a soufflé a surprise centre by adding an ingredient that needs brief, light cooking, such as fish or cooked vegetables. Try adding chunks of boned, skinned salmon or smoked haddock to a light cheese and herb soufflé. Spoon half the soufflé mixture into the dish. Add the fish and spoon the rest of the mixture over the top. Cook as usual.

To give a soufflé a cracked top or top-hat effect, make a deep cut in the top of the mixture with a spoon or knife.

Making a Cold or Iced Soufflé

1 Prepare a soufflé dish with a collar. Make 450ml/¾ pint/scant 2 cups thick custard and pour into a large bowl. Set aside to cool.

2 Dissolve 15ml/1 tbsp powdered gelatine in 45ml/3tbsp water and blend with the chosen flavouring, such as coffee essence, mocha syrup or sieved crushed fruit, and stir into the custard. Mix well until the flavouring is evenly blended with the custard. Chill.

3 When the mixture is beginning to set, whisk the egg whites with the caster (superfine) sugar as for meringue.

4 Fold the meringue into the custard mixture. Use a large balloon whisk for folding in because it will help to break up the meringue more evenly and blend the two textures.

5 When the mixture is nearly set, carefully pour it into the prepared dish or tin. The mixture should come about 5cm/2in above the rim. Chill until set or freeze for at least 1 hour before serving to make an iced soufflé.

6 When ready to serve the soufflé, carefully, and very slowly, peel off the paper collar. If the paper does not come away easily, use a warm, round-bladed knife to start it off.

7 Coat the side of the soufflé with chocolate or chopped toasted nuts. Press the coating on the soufflé using a cake slice. Decorate the top with piped cream and/or more chocolate.

Cold Savoury Soufflés

These can be made by the same basic method as a cold sweet soufflé, using a plain savoury sauce or purée of ingredients as the base. Dissolve the gelatine into the flavouring mixture, stir into the savoury sauce, then allow to part-set before folding in the egg whites.

Coating the soufflé dish

To give hot or cold soufflés additional flavour, the inside of the dish can be coated before adding the mixture. Grated chocolate complements a sweet coffee soufflé. For a savoury soufflé, try using grated Parmesan cheese or fine breadcrumbs: plain white breadcrumbs can be used when making a baked soufflé, and toasted breadcrumbs complement a chilled soufflé. Butter the dish, then shake the coating liberally all over the inside. Tip out any excess.

PASTRY

Eggs are often used to enrich pastry. They help to bind the dry ingredients together, make the pastry more pliable and give a rich crumbly result. Whole egg can be used but it is more common to use just the yolk as the white can give a tough result. Eggs are also a key ingredient for choux pastry in which they act as the setting agent and, along with air, help the pastry to rise.

Making Rich Shortcrust Pastry

Rub together 115g/4oz/1 cup butter, into 225g/8oz/2 cups plain (all-purpose) flour. Blend in 1 egg yolk and a little cold water, then mix thoroughly to form a smooth dough. Chill for about 10 minutes.

Making Rich Cheese Pastry

This delicious savoury pastry is perfect for all occasions. It uses cream cheese as well as butter.

Sift 225g/8oz/2 cups plain (all-purpose) flour and a pinch of salt on to a work surface or a large bowl. Add 75g/3oz/6 tbsp each of soft butter and soft cream cheese and 1–2 egg yolks. Rub together the mixture with your fingers, until a thick paste forms. Chill for 10 minutes.

Making Choux Pastry

This pastry is the base for éclairs and profiteroles. It is also used for savoury pastries such as gougère, a filled ring of choux pastry, and aigrettes, which are deep fried cheese choux buns. When the pastry cooks, it fills with air, creating a hollow that is perfect for filling.

1 Sift 65g/2½oz/9 tbsp plain (all-purpose) flour and a pinch of salt on to a sheet of greaseproof (waxed) paper.

2 Melt 50g/2oz/4 tbsp butter in a small saucepan with 150ml/¼ pint/⅔ cup cold water. Bring to a rolling boil, then remove from the heat.

3 Tip the sifted flour into the pan all at once and beat together quickly to make a stiff paste that comes away from the sides of the pan in a ball. Do not beat hard or the paste will become oily. Leave to cool slightly.

4 Gradually pour 3 beaten eggs into the paste, beating hard to combine after each addition.

5 The mixture will be slightly lumpy at first, but keep beating hard until the egg and paste are thoroughly mixed and have a smooth and glossy texture.

6 If the paste is too firm, add an additional 15–30ml/1–2 tbsp beaten egg to the mixture. It should have a firm dropping consistency.

7 Line a baking sheet with non-stick baking paper or grease it well. To make profiteroles, use two teaspoons to place small quantities of choux paste on the prepared baking sheet, spacing them well apart.

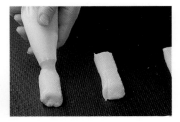

8 To make éclairs, place the paste in a piping bag without a nozzle and pipe 5cm/2in long cylinders well apart in neat lines.

9 Preheat the oven to 200°C/400°F/ Gas 6. Bake medium-size buns for 20–25 minutes; smaller buns for a few minutes less; éclairs for 30–35 minutes and larger rings for 40–45 minutes.

SAVOURY ROULADES

These are based on the basic savoury soufflé mixture, which is then baked in a Swiss roll tin (jelly roll pan).

Making a Savoury Roulade

1 Grease and lightly dust the tin or line with baking parchment. Preheat the oven to 190°C/375°F/Gas 5.

2 Melt 25g/1oz/2 tbsp butter in a pan and blend in 25g/1oz/¼ cup plain (all-purpose) flour. Whisk in 300ml/½ pint/1¼ cups warm milk and bring to the boil, whisking until thickened. Cool slightly, then add to 4 beaten egg yolks.

3 Stir in flavouring ingredients, such as well-seasoned spinach purée or cheese.

4 Whisk 4 egg whites stiffly, then fold in the sauce, until evenly blended.

5 Pour the mixture into the prepared tin and spread it evenly into the corners. Bake for 10–12 minutes, or until just firm to the touch. If it is overcooked, the edges become too crisp and the roulade will not roll easily.

6 While the roulade is cooking, lay a sheet of greaseproof (waxed) paper on a clean dish towel. Sprinkle with finely grated Parmesan cheese, if you wish. Invert the hot roulade on to the paper and leave to cool slightly before removing the lining paper.

7 Savoury mixtures are best rolled up while hot, but they can also be rolled as they cool. Roll up the roulade using the dish towel and paper as support. Wrap the roulade in the dish towel to keep it moist until you are ready to unroll it and add the filling.

WHISKED SPONGES

These incredibly light sponges have an open airy texture. They can be plain or flavoured and baked in layers or fingers, or in thin rectangles for making Swiss rolls and roulades. Luscious or light fillings can be added after cooking. The sponge can be made without fat, or melted butter can be added, as for Genoese sponge; allow about 15g/½oz/1 tbsp butter per egg. This will give a richer, slightly more dense sponge with better keeping qualities. Fatless sponges become stale very quickly, so are best used on the day they are made; however, they do freeze well. Sponge with added butter will keep in an airtight container for 1–2 days.

Preparing tins

A sponge sandwich tin or a deep cake tin should be greased and dusted lightly with flour. The thin flour coating provides a surface to which the light mixture clings as it rises and this helps to give a neat straight side on the baked sponge. If you are concerned that the sponge may stick to the base of the tin, then line it with baking parchment after greasing and flouring the sides. This will also help to support the cake when it is turned out.

To prepare a Swiss roll tin, cut a sheet of greaseproof (waxed) paper 2.5cm/1in larger than the tin on all sides. Stand the tin on the paper and draw around its base. Use scissors to snip into the corners. Place the paper in the tin, overlapping the corners neatly.

Making a Whisked Sponge

Whisking the mixture over hot water helps to make a far lighter sponge.

1 Grease and lightly dust the tin or line with non-stick baking paper. Preheat the oven to 190°C/375°F/Gas 5.

2 Using an electric beater, whisk the eggs and sugar in a large heatproof bowl over a saucepan of simmering water.

3 Continue whisking until the mixture is very pale, fluffy and thick. The sponge mixture should hold a trail when you lift out the whisk. Remove the bowl from the heat and continue to whisk until the mixture cools.

4 Sift the flour twice, then fold it into the whisked mixture. Fold in the melted butter, if using.

5 Continue folding very gently with a large spatula until thoroughly mixed. Pour the sponge mixture into the prepared tins. Bake for 10–12 minutes until well risen and springy to touch.

Making a Swiss Roll

These are made from a light whisked sponge cooked in a Swiss roll tin. The prepared sponge should be rolled up while still warm to prevent it cracking.

1 While the sponge is cooking lay a clean sheet of greaseproof paper on a clean dish towel. Sprinkle with caster (superfine) or icing (confectioners') sugar.

2 Gently invert the sponge on to the centre of the paper, then slowly peel off the lining paper. If the paper does not come away easily, use a rounded knife to ease the paper from the sponge.

3 Trim the edges using a sharp knife, then make a shallow cut 2.5cm/1in from one short side of the cake to help it begin to roll.

4 Roll up the cake while it is still warm, using the towel as support. Leave the greaseproof paper inside so the sponge does not stick to itself while cooling. Set aside to cool.

5 Carefully unroll the sponge, spread with jam and cream or your chosen filling, then carefully roll up again.

Sweet roulades

These can be made with other mixtures, such as meringue or a rich chocolate mixture, but are always cooked in a Swiss roll tin.

Piping Meringue

The stiff texture of meringue is perfect for piping. Small meringue rosettes can be used to decorate desserts or serve with fruit; nests can be filled with fruit, flavoured creams or ice cream.

1 Fit a star nozzle in a large piping bag and fill with meringue. To pipe rosettes, make one swirling motion, then pipe across and around again. Lift up the nozzle sharply to make a neat peak.

2 To make nests, use a star nozzle and pipe using a swirling motion to make the base. Then pipe a top outer rim to make sides for the nest.

3 To make the base of a meringue gâteau or Vacherin, use a plain or fluted nozzle and pipe a continuous spiral of meringue to form a large round.

4 To top an open tart filled with apple or lemon with meringue, pipe meringue in a neat lattice design.

5 Alternatively, pipe very small rosettes all the way round the edge of an open tart or pie.

Cooking meringue toppings

Any open tart or pie is delicious topped with piped meringue. A sweet, mouthwatering meringue topping complements a slightly sharp filling, such as gooseberries, rhubarb, blackberries or lemon curd, perfectly.

Meringue toppings are quite different from dry meringue and need to be cooked in a different way. They should be cooked at a much higher temperature, to give a crisp light brown outside of caramelized sugar, and a soft mallowy inside.

Start cooking the tart or pie and, when it is nearly cooked, spoon or pipe the meringue over the filling. Return to the oven and cook at 200°C/400°F/Gas 6 for a further 7–8 minutes or until golden brown and crisp.

Making Meringue Rounds

Layers of crunchy meringue sandwiched with fruit and/or cream fillings make a stunning dessert. Toasted nuts give the best flavour. Try hazelnuts or almonds and chop them finely as they give a good crunchy texture superior to that obtained by grinding the nuts finely. Line two or more baking sheets with baking parchment. It helps to draw a circle on the reverse of the paper in heavy pencil, then use it as a guide when spreading the meringue.

1 Fold the toasted nuts evenly and gently into the prepared meringue.

2 Gently spread the nutty meringue mixture evenly into flat circles about 20–22.5cm/8–9in in diameter on the prepared baking sheets.

PAVLOVA

This much loved dessert is a delicious variation on the meringue theme. Pavlova has a crisp outer layer that conceals a soft and chewy centre. It is usually filled with cream and fresh fruits and makes a luxurious finale to a dinner party.

The dessert is thought to have originated in Australia, created by a chef in Perth. Named after the Russian ballerina Anna Pavlova who visited Australia in 1926, the fluffy meringue sides are thought to represent the ballerina's tutu.

Pavlova is surprisingly easy to make and can be made in advance and stored in an airtight tin for several days. Although every cook seems to have their own secret for attaining the prized mallowy centre, there are three main elements during preparation that make pavlova different from other meringues: the addition of cornflour (cornstarch) and vinegar; folding in the sugar, and the depth of the cooked meringue. These key differences in the dessert's preparation help to create the softer, chewier centre.

Pavlova fillings

There are a great many variations on the traditional pavlova, though the most authentic fruit filling is thought to be passion fruit. Many colours and combinations of fruits can be used or, alternatively, chopped fruit can be mixed into the whipped cream. The cream can also be flavoured with lemon curd to give a tangier flavour, or a teaspoon of brandy or liqueur can be stirred in at the last minute.

The fruit can be substituted entirely, if wished, and replaced with grated or chipped chocolate or crushed ratafia biscuits.

The meringue shell can be sprinkled with flaked (sliced) almonds, shredded coconut, cocoa powder or grated chocolate halfway through cooking to add extra flavour and texture.

Making Pavlova

1 Start by making a traditional meringue mixture using 4 egg whites but do not whisk in all of the sugar. Sift 15–30ml/1–2 tbsp cornflour (cornstarch) over the meringue, then fold in the last of the sugar. The amount of cornflour depends on the number of egg whites used.

2 Add 15ml/1 tbsp light vinegar such as white wine vinegar or distilled white vinegar.

COOK'S TIP

When filling a pavlova, always make sure that the serving plate is completely flat. The weight of the filling may cause the pavlova to sink into a slightly curved dish, cracking the crisp outer layer of the pavlova beyond repair.

If you do have a disaster when making a pavlova, combine the broken pieces of meringue with cream and fruit and freeze for several hours to make a delicous soft-scoop ice cream.

3 Use a large metal spoon or plastic spatula to cut through the mixture and fold it over, incorporating the vinegar until evenly blended. Work very gently to avoid knocking out any of the air from the meringue.

4 Preheat the oven to 140°C/275°F/Gas 1. Prepare 1 baking sheet, drawing a 23cm/9in circle in heavy pencil on the reverse of the paper.

5 Spread half the mixture into a thick, flat neat round, then spoon the rest in high swirls around the edge to create a border. Add to the border to give more height if you have any extra meringue mixture. Bake for 1–1½ hours until the meringue is firm, checking frequently to avoid the meringue overcooking and turning brown.

6 When cooked and cooled, peel off the paper and fill the pavlova shell with whipped cream and fresh fruit.

COOKING WITH EGGS

Eggs are both delicious and versatile, and can be used in a huge range of dishes. They are wonderful served on their own — poached, boiled, fried or scrambled — but they can also create exciting and unusual dishes when combined with other ingredients. Light and fluffy soufflés, crisp meringues, succulent cakes and moist omelettes are just a few of the mouthwatering dishes that can be made with eggs.

BREAKFASTS AND BRUNCHES

Eggs first became an important breakfast food in the Victorian era.
Nowadays, eggs have become a key ingredient, both for breakfasts and lazy
weekend brunches, and are used to create enticing dishes that are a far cry
from plain boiled eggs or poached eggs on toast.
Eggs make a perfect start to the day, providing plenty of energy to keep you
going. This chapter includes classic breakfast and brunch dishes, such as
Poached Eggs Florentine, Scrambled Eggs with Smoked Salmon, and
Bacon, Egg and Chanterelle Baps, as well as more
unusual recipes, such as Shirred Eggs with
Pancetta and Rocket, and Stuffed
Thai Omelette.

EGGS BENEDICT

THERE IS STILL DEBATE OVER WHO CREATED THIS RECIPE BUT THE MOST LIKELY STORY CREDITS MR AND MRS LEGRAND BENEDICT, REGULARS AT NEW YORK'S DELMONICO'S RESTAURANT, WHO COMPLAINED THERE WAS NOTHING NEW ON THE LUNCH MENU. THIS DISH WAS CREATED AS A RESULT.

SERVES FOUR

INGREDIENTS
  4 eggs
  2 English muffins or 4 slices
    of bread
  butter, for spreading
  4 thick slices cooked ham, cut
    to fit the muffins
  fresh chives, to garnish
For the sauce
  3 egg yolks
  30ml/2 tbsp fresh lemon juice
  1.5ml/¼ tsp salt
  115g/4oz/½ cup butter
  30ml/2 tbsp single (light) cream
  ground black pepper

COOK'S TIP
Use only very fresh eggs for poaching, because they keep their shape better in the water.

1 To make the sauce, blend the egg yolks, lemon juice and salt in a food processor or blender for 15 seconds.

2 Melt the butter in a small pan until it bubbles, but do not let it brown. With the motor running, slowly pour the hot butter into the food processor or blender through the feed tube in a slow, steady stream. Turn off the machine as soon as all the butter has been added.

3 Pour the sauce into a bowl, placed over a pan of simmering water. Stir for 2–3 minutes, until thickened. If the sauce begins to curdle, whisk in 15ml/ 1 tbsp boiling water. Stir in the cream and season with pepper. Remove from the heat and keep warm over the pan.

4 Bring a shallow pan of lightly salted water to the boil. Break each egg into a cup, then slide it carefully into the water. Delicately turn the white around the yolk with a spoon. Cook for about 4 minutes until the white is set. Remove the eggs from the pan, one at a time, using a slotted spoon, and drain on kitchen paper. Cut off any ragged edges with a small knife or scissors.

5 While the eggs are poaching, split and toast the muffins or toast the slices of bread. Spread with butter while still warm.

6 Place a piece of ham, which you may brown in butter if you wish, on each muffin half or slice of toast, then place an egg on each ham-topped muffin. Spoon the warm sauce over the eggs, garnish with chives and serve.

POACHED EGGS FLORENTINE

FLORENTINE DISHES, WHICH ARE COOKED IN "THE STYLE OF FLORENCE", ALWAYS CONTAIN SPINACH AND MAY ALSO BE TOPPED WITH A CREAMY SAUCE.

SERVES FOUR

INGREDIENTS
   675g/1½lb spinach, washed
      and drained
   25g/1oz/2 tbsp butter
   60ml/4 tbsp double (heavy) cream
   pinch of freshly grated nutmeg
For the topping
   25g/1oz/2 tbsp butter
   25g/1oz/¼ cup plain
      (all-purpose) flour
   300ml/½ pint/1¼ cups hot milk
   pinch of ground mace
   115g/4oz/1 cup Gruyère cheese, grated
   4 eggs
   15ml/1 tbsp freshly grated
      Parmesan cheese
   salt and ground black pepper

COOK'S TIP
This dish can be prepared with any other green vegetable that is in season, such as chard, fennel or Chinese cabbage.

1 Preheat the oven to 200°C/400°F/ Gas 6. Place the spinach in a large pan with a little water. Cook for 3–4 minutes, then drain well and chop finely. Return to the pan, add the butter, cream, nutmeg and seasoning, and heat through. Spoon into four small gratin dishes, making a well in the middle of each.

2 To make the topping, heat the butter in a small pan, add the flour and cook for 1 minute, stirring. Gradually blend in the hot milk, beating well.

3 Cook for 2 minutes, stirring. Remove from the heat and stir in the mace and 75g/3oz/¾ cup of the Gruyère cheese.

4 Break each egg into a cup and slide it into a pan of lightly salted simmering water. Poach for 3–4 minutes. Lift out the eggs using a slotted spoon and drain on kitchen paper. Place a poached egg in the middle of each dish and cover with the cheese sauce. Sprinkle with the remaining cheeses and bake for 10 minutes or until just golden.

SWEET PERSIAN BREAKFAST OMELETTE

THIS VERSION OF A SIMPLE OMELETTE IS POPULAR THROUGHOUT THE MIDDLE EAST AND IS EXCELLENT EATEN WITH A FRUITY HOME-MADE JAM OR CONSERVE.

SERVES ONE

INGREDIENTS
3 eggs
10ml/2 tsp caster (superfine) sugar
5ml/1 tsp plain (all-purpose) flour
10g/¼oz/½ tbsp unsalted butter
bread and jam, to serve

COOK'S TIP
Continue the Middle Eastern theme when choosing a jam to serve with this omelette. Pick a conserve made from fruits such as fig or apricot that are popular in the Middle East. Alternatively, use raspberry or strawberry jam, which will be just as good.

1 Break the eggs into a large bowl, add the sugar and flour and beat until really frothy. Heat the butter in an omelette pan until it begins to bubble, then pour in the egg mixture and cook, without stirring, until it begins to set.

2 Run a wooden spatula around the edge of the omelette, then carefully turn it over and cook the second side for 1–2 minutes until golden. Serve hot or warm with thick slices of fresh bread and fruity jam.

CHIVE SCRAMBLED EGGS IN BRIOCHES

SCRAMBLED EGGS ARE DELICIOUS AT ANY TIME OF DAY BUT, WHEN SERVED WITH FRANCE'S FAVOURITE BREAKFAST BREAD, THEY BECOME THE ULTIMATE BREAKFAST OR BRUNCH TREAT. THESE SCRAMBLED EGGS ARE SOFTER AND CREAMIER THAN OTHER VERSIONS, AND TASTE GOOD SERVED COLD.

SERVES FOUR

INGREDIENTS
4 individual brioches
6 eggs, beaten
30ml/2 tbsp snipped fresh chives, plus extra to serve
25g/1oz/2 tbsp butter
45ml/3 tbsp cottage cheese
60–75ml/4–5 tbsp double (heavy) cream
salt and ground black pepper

1 Preheat the oven to 180°C/350°F/ Gas 4. Cut the tops off the brioches and set to one side. Carefully scoop out the centre of each brioche, leaving a bread case. Put the brioche cases and lids on a baking sheet and bake for 5 minutes until hot and crisp.

COOK'S TIP
Save the scooped-out brioche centres and freeze them in an airtight container. Partly defrost and blend or grate them to make crumbs for coating fish or pieces of chicken before frying.

2 Lightly beat the eggs and season to taste. Add about half the chives. Heat the butter in a medium pan until it begins to foam, then add the eggs and cook, stirring with a wooden spoon until semi-solid.

3 Stir in the cottage cheese, cream and the rest of the chives, and continue to cook for 1–2 minutes, making sure that the eggs remain soft and creamy.

4 To serve, spoon the eggs into the crisp brioche shells and sprinkle with the extra chives.

COOK'S TIP
If you do not happen to have brioches to hand, these wonderful herby eggs taste delicious on top of thick slices of toasted bread. Try them piled high on warm focaccia, or on toasted ciabatta, granary bread or muffins.

SAVOURY SCRAMBLED EGGS

ALSO KNOWN AS "SCOTCH WOODCOCK", THESE EGGS ARE FLAVOURED WITH A HINT OF ANCHOVY AND WERE POPULAR IN ENGLAND AT THE BEGINNING OF THE 20TH CENTURY. THEY WOULD HAVE BEEN SERVED AS A SAVOURY INSTEAD OF CHEESE AT THE END OF A MEAL RATHER THAN FOR BREAKFAST.

SERVES TWO

INGREDIENTS
  2 slices bread
  40g/1½oz/3 tbsp butter, plus
    extra for spreading
  anchovy paste, such as
    Gentleman's Relish, for spreading
  2 eggs and 2 egg yolks, beaten
  60–90ml/4–6 tbsp cream
    or milk
  salt and ground black pepper
  anchovy fillets, cut into strips,
    and paprika, to garnish

COOK'S TIP
These creamy scrambled eggs make a great brunch dish. Serve with a glass of crisp white wine and follow with a fresh fruit salad.

1 Toast the bread, spread with butter and anchovy paste, then remove the crusts and cut into triangles. Keep warm.

2 Melt the rest of the butter in a medium non-stick saucepan, then stir in the beaten eggs, cream or milk, and a little salt and pepper. Heat very gently, stirring constantly, until the mixture begins to thicken.

3 Remove the saucepan from the heat and continue to stir until the mixture becomes very creamy, but do not allow it to harden.

4 Divide the scrambled eggs among the triangles of toast and garnish each one with strips of anchovy fillet and a generous sprinkling of paprika. Serve immediately, while still hot.

PIPÉRADE WITH CROSTINI

THIS MIXTURE OF SWEET PEPPERS, TOMATOES AND EGGS HAS ALL THE FLAVOURS OF THE
MEDITERRANEAN. IT IS PERFECT FOR A LAZY WEEKEND BRUNCH OR A LIGHT LUNCH-TIME SNACK.

SERVES SIX

INGREDIENTS
  60ml/4 tbsp bacon fat, duck fat
    or olive oil
  2 small onions, coarsely chopped
  4 red, orange or yellow (bell)
    peppers, seeded and chopped
  2 large garlic cloves, finely chopped
  pinch of chilli or hot cayenne pepper
  675g/1½lb ripe plum tomatoes,
    peeled, seeded and chopped
  15ml/1 tbsp chopped fresh oregano
    or 5ml/1 tsp dried
  1 long French stick
  60–90ml/4–6 tbsp olive oil
  25g/1oz/2 tbsp butter
  6 eggs, beaten
  salt and ground black pepper
  basil leaves, to serve

1 Heat the fat or oil in a large heavy-based frying pan. Add the onions and cook over a gentle heat, stirring occasionally, for about 5 minutes until softened but not coloured.

2 Add the peppers, garlic and chilli or cayenne. Cook for a further 5 minutes, stirring, then add the plum tomatoes, seasoning and oregano, and cook over a moderate heat for 15–20 minutes until the peppers are soft and most of the liquid has evaporated.

COOK'S TIP
To make a quick party version, cut the bread into thick slices and mix about 200ml/7fl oz/scant 1 cup ready-made sweet pepper and tomato pasta sauce into the eggs and continue as above.

3 Preheat the oven to 200°C/400°F/ Gas 6. Cut the bread in half lengthways, trim off the ends, then cut into six equal pieces and brush with olive oil. Place on baking trays and bake for 8–10 minutes until crisp and just turning golden.

4 Heat the butter until it bubbles, add the eggs and stir until softly scrambled. Turn off the heat and stir in the pepper mixture. Divide evenly among the pieces of bread and sprinkle with the basil leaves. Serve hot or warm.

SCRAMBLED EGGS WITH SMOKED SALMON

FOR A LUXURY BREAKFAST, OR A LATE-NIGHT SUPPER, YOU CAN'T BEAT THIS VERY SPECIAL COMBINATION. TRY IT ON CHRISTMAS MORNING ALONG WITH A GLASS OF CHAMPAGNE MIXED WITH FRESHLY SQUEEZED ORANGE JUICE.

SERVES FOUR

INGREDIENTS
    4 slices of pumpernickel or
        wholemeal bread, crusts trimmed
    50g/2oz/4 tbsp butter
    115g/4oz sliced smoked salmon
    6 eggs
    45–60ml/3–4 tbsp double
        (heavy) cream
    60ml/4 tbsp crème fraîche
    salt and ground black pepper
    generous 60ml/4 tbsp lumpfish roe
        or salmon caviar and sprigs of dill,
        to garnish

COOK'S TIP
If you are lucky enough to have a truffle, then another real treat is to grate a little fresh truffle into the scrambled eggs. Serve them on toast, topped with a little chopped fresh chervil.

1 Spread the slices of bread with half of the butter and arrange the smoked salmon on top. Cut each slice in half and set aside while you make the scrambled eggs.

2 Lightly beat the eggs together and season with salt and freshly ground pepper. Melt the remaining butter in a pan until sizzling, then quickly stir in the beaten eggs.

3 Stir constantly until the eggs begin to thicken. Just before they have finished cooking, stir in the cream. Remove the saucepan from the heat and stir in the crème fraîche. Set the eggs aside and keep warm.

4 Spoon the scrambled eggs on to the smoked salmon. Top each serving with a spoonful of caviar and serve, garnished with sprigs of dill.

EGG CROSTINI WITH ROUILLE

CROSTINI ARE EXTREMELY QUICK TO MAKE SO ARE PERFECT FOR BREAKFAST OR BRUNCH. THE ROUILLE GIVES THEM A HINT OF MEDITERRANEAN FLAVOUR. TRADITIONALLY, ROUILLE IS SERVED WITH THICK FISH SOUP, BUT HERE IT PROVIDES THE PERFECT COMPLEMENT TO LIGHTLY FRIED EGGS.

SERVES FOUR

INGREDIENTS
    4 slices of ciabatta bread
    extra virgin olive oil
    45ml/3 tbsp home-made mayonnaise
    5ml/1 tsp harissa
    4 eggs
    4 small slices smoked ham
    watercress, to serve

COOK'S TIP
Harissa is a fiery North African chilli paste made from dried red chillies, cumin, garlic, coriander, caraway and olive oil. It adds a sweet spicy taste to dips, sauces and stews, and makes a great addition to mayonnaise for serving with meat or fish dishes.

1 Preheat the oven to 200°C/400°F/ Gas 6. Use a pastry brush to lightly brush each slice of ciabatta bread with a little olive oil. Place the bread on a baking sheet and bake for 10 minutes or until crisp and turning golden brown.

2 Meanwhile, make the rouille. Mix together the mayonnaise and harissa. Fry the eggs lightly in a very little oil in a non-stick pan.

3 Top the baked bread with the ham, eggs and a small spoonful of rouille. Serve immediately with watercress.

BACON, EGG AND CHANTERELLE BAPS

THE DELICATE CHANTERELLE MUSHROOM WITH ITS SLIGHT FRUITINESS COMBINES BEAUTIFULLY WITH EGGS AND BACON FOR THIS RATHER SOPHISTICATED BREAKFAST BAP.

SERVES FOUR

INGREDIENTS

   350g/12oz unsmoked
     bacon rashers (strips)
   50g/2oz/4 tbsp unsalted butter,
     plus extra for spreading
   115g/4oz/1½ cups chanterelle
     mushrooms, trimmed and halved
   60ml/4 tbsp sunflower oil
   4 eggs
   4 large baps, split
   salt and ground black pepper

COOK'S TIP
Other varieties of mushroom can be used instead of chanterelles. Try brown cap (cremini) mushrooms, chestnut mushrooms or freshly picked field (portobello) mushrooms.

1 Place the bacon in a large non-stick frying pan and fry in its own fat until crisp. Transfer to a heatproof plate, cover and keep warm in a low oven.

2 Melt 25g/1oz/2 tbsp of the butter in the pan, add the chanterelles and fry over a gentle heat until soft, without letting them colour. Transfer to a plate, cover and keep warm.

3 Melt the remaining butter, add the oil and heat to a moderate temperature. Break the eggs into the pan, two at a time, if necessary. Fry them, turning to cook both sides if you like.

4 Toast the baps, spread with butter, then top each with bacon, chanterelles and a fried egg. Season, add the bap lids and serve at once.

AMERICAN PANCAKES WITH GRILLED BACON

THESE SMALL, THICK, BUTTERY PANCAKES WILL BE EATEN IN SECONDS, SO MAKE PLENTY. THE BATTER CAN BE MADE THE NIGHT BEFORE, READY FOR BREAKFAST.

MAKES ABOUT TWENTY

INGREDIENTS

175g/6oz/1½ cups plain (all-purpose)
  flour, sifted
pinch of salt
15ml/1 tbsp caster (superfine) sugar
2 large eggs
150ml/¼ pint/⅔ cup milk
5ml/1 tsp bicarbonate of soda
  (baking soda)
10ml/2 tsp cream of tartar
oil, for cooking
butter, maple syrup and crisply
  grilled (broiled) bacon, to serve

COOK'S TIP
Make pancakes in advance and freeze.

1 To make the batter, mix together the flour, salt and sugar. In a separate bowl, beat the eggs and milk together, then gradually stir into the flour, beating to a smooth, thick consistency. Add the bicarbonate of soda and cream of tartar, mix well, then cover and chill until ready to cook.

2 When you are ready to cook the pancakes, beat the batter again. Heat a little oil in a heavy-based frying pan or griddle. Drop dessertspoonfuls of the mixture into the pan, spaced well apart, and cook over a fairly high heat until bubbles appear on the surface of the pancakes and the undersides become golden brown.

3 Carefully turn the pancakes over with a palette knife or fish slice and cook briefly until golden underneath, then transfer them to a heated serving dish. Top each pancake with a little butter and drizzle with maple syrup. Serve with grilled bacon.

OMELETTE ARNOLD BENNETT

CREATED FOR THE AUTHOR, ARNOLD BENNETT, WHO FREQUENTLY DINED AT THE SAVOY HOTEL IN LONDON, THIS CREAMY, SMOKED HADDOCK SOUFFLÉ OMELETTE IS NOW SERVED ALL OVER THE WORLD.

SERVES TWO

INGREDIENTS

175g/6oz smoked haddock fillet,
  poached and drained
50g/2oz/4 tbsp butter, diced
175ml/6fl oz/¾ cup whipping or
  double (heavy) cream
4 eggs, separated
40g/1½oz/⅓ cup mature (sharp)
  Cheddar cheese, grated
ground black pepper
watercress or rocket (arugula),
  to garnish

COOK'S TIP

Try to buy smoked haddock that does not contain artificial colouring for this recipe. Besides being better for you, it gives the omelette a lighter, more attractive colour.

1 Remove the skin and any bones from the haddock fillet and discard. Carefully flake the flesh using a fork.

2 Melt half the butter with 60ml/4 tbsp of the cream in a fairly small non-stick pan, then add the flaked fish and stir together gently. Cover the pan with a lid, remove from the heat and set aside to cool.

3 Mix the egg yolks with 15ml/1 tbsp of the cream. Season with pepper, then stir into the fish. In a separate bowl, mix the cheese and the remaining cream. Stiffly whisk the egg whites, then fold into the fish mixture. Heat the remaining butter in an omelette pan, add the fish mixture and cook until browned underneath. Pour the cheese mixture over and grill until bubbling. Garnish and serve.

SOUFFLÉ OMELETTE <u>WITH</u> MUSHROOMS

A SOUFFLÉ OMELETTE MAKES AN IDEAL MEAL FOR ONE, ESPECIALLY WITH THIS DELICIOUS FILLING.
USE A COMBINATION OF DIFFERENT MUSHROOMS, SUCH AS OYSTER OR CHESTNUT, IF YOU LIKE.

SERVES ONE

INGREDIENTS
  2 eggs, separated
  15g/½oz/1 tbsp butter
  flat leaf parsley or coriander
    (cilantro) leaves, to garnish
For the mushroom sauce
  15g/½oz/1 tbsp butter
  75g/3oz/generous 1 cup button
    (white) mushrooms, thinly sliced
  15ml/1 tbsp plain (all-purpose) flour
  85–120ml/3–4fl oz/⅓–½ cup milk
  5ml/1 tsp chopped fresh flat leaf
    parsley (optional)
  salt and ground black pepper

1 To make the mushroom sauce, melt the butter in a saucepan or frying pan and add the sliced mushrooms. Fry gently for 4–5 minutes, stirring occasionally, until tender.

2 Stir in the flour, then gradually add the milk, stirring all the time. Cook until boiling and thickened. Add the parsley, if using, and season with salt and pepper. Keep warm.

3 Beat the egg yolks with 15ml/1 tbsp water and season with a little salt and pepper. Whisk the egg whites until stiff, then fold into the egg yolks using a metal spoon. Preheat the grill (broiler).

4 Melt the butter in a large frying pan and pour the egg mixture into the pan. Cook over a gentle heat for 2–4 minutes. Place the frying pan under the grill and cook for a further 3–4 minutes until the top is golden brown.

5 Slide the omelette on to a warmed serving plate, pour the mushroom sauce over the top and fold the omelette in half. Serve, garnished with parsley or coriander leaves.

COOK'S TIP
For extra flavour, add a few drops of Worcestershire sauce to the mushrooms as they cook.

SHIRRED EGGS WITH PANCETTA AND ROCKET

THESE EGGS ARE BAKED WITH ITALIAN BACON IN INDIVIDUAL OVENPROOF DISHES. YOU COULD ADD OTHER INGREDIENTS, SUCH AS SPICY SAUSAGE OR SAUTÉED SPINACH.

SERVES FOUR

INGREDIENTS
  50g/2oz/4 tbsp butter
  115g/4oz pancetta, sliced
  8 eggs
  bunch of rocket (arugula)
  squeeze of lemon juice
  15ml/1 tbsp olive oil
  ground black pepper

COOK'S TIP
For hungry guests, use very large double-yolk eggs for this dish and serve with lots of freshly baked ciabatta bread spread with unsalted butter.

1 Preheat the oven to 200°C/400°F/ Gas 6. Divide half the butter and all of the pancetta among four individual serving or gratin dishes.

2 Bake for 8–10 minutes until the pancetta is sizzling, then carefully remove the dishes from the oven.

3 Crack two eggs into each dish, add another knob of butter to each and sprinkle with seasoning. Return to the oven for a further 7–8 minutes or until the eggs are just set.

4 Toss the rocket in the lemon juice and oil, and add some to each dish.

TOMATO AND COURGETTE TIMBALES

THESE BAKED SAVOURY CUSTARDS ARE TYPICAL OF SOUTHERN FRENCH COOKING. THE EGG AND VEGETABLE COMBINATION IS DELICIOUS; SERVE WARM OR COOL AS A LIGHT MEAL, AN ACCOMPANIMENT TO A MAIN MEAL, OR A STARTER.

SERVES FOUR

INGREDIENTS
  a little butter
  2 courgettes (zucchini)
  2 firm, ripe vine tomatoes, sliced
  2 eggs and 2 egg yolks
  45ml/3 tbsp double (heavy) cream
  15ml/1 tbsp fresh tomato sauce or
    passata (bottled strained tomatoes)
  10ml/2 tsp chopped fresh basil or
    oregano or 5ml/1 tsp dried
  salt and ground black pepper
  sautéed potatoes, to serve

VARIATIONS
Replace the courgettes (zucchini) with chopped asparagus or aubergine (eggplant) if you prefer. Steam the asparagus for 3–7 minutes and the aubergine for 3–4 minutes.

1 Preheat the oven to 180°C/350°F/ Gas 4. Lightly butter four large ramekins or individual ovenproof dishes.

2 Top and tail the courgettes, then cut them into thin slices. Put them into a steamer, place over a pan of boiling water, cover with a lid and steam for 4–5 minutes. Shake the steamer to get rid of as much moisture as possible, then layer the courgettes in the ramekins with the sliced tomatoes.

3 Whisk together the eggs, cream, tomato sauce or passata, herbs and seasoning. Pour the egg mixture into the ramekins, dividing it evenly. Place in a roasting tin (pan) and half fill the tin with hot water. Bake for 20–30 minutes until the custard is just firm.

4 Cool slightly then run a knife around the rims. Carefully turn out on to small plates. Serve with sautéed potatoes.

SOFT TACOS WITH SPICED OMELETTE

SERVED HOT, WARM OR COLD, THESE TACOS MAKE EASY FOOD ON THE MOVE FOR YOUNGER MEMBERS OF THE FAMILY, WHEN THEY NEED SOMETHING NOURISHING TO TAKE ON A PICNIC, HIKE OR CYCLE RIDE.

SERVES FOUR

INGREDIENTS
30ml/2 tbsp sunflower oil
50g/2oz beansprouts
50g/2oz carrots, cut into
    thin sticks
25g/1oz Chinese cabbage, chopped
15ml/1 tbsp light soy sauce
4 eggs
1 small spring onion (scallion),
    finely sliced
5ml/1 tsp Cajun seasoning
25g/1oz/2 tbsp butter
4 soft flour tortillas, warmed in
    the oven or microwave
salt and ground black pepper

COOK'S TIP
You can buy fresh soft tortillas in large supermarkets. They freeze well, so keep a packet or two in the freezer.

1 Heat the oil in a small frying pan and stir-fry the beansprouts, carrot sticks and chopped cabbage until they begin to soften. Add the soy sauce, stir to combine and set aside.

2 Place the eggs, sliced spring onion, Cajun seasoning, salt and ground black pepper in a bowl, and beat together. Melt the butter in a small pan until it sizzles. Add the beaten eggs and cook over a gentle heat, stirring constantly, until almost firm.

3 Divide the vegetables and scrambled egg evenly among the tortillas, fold up into cones or parcels and serve. For travelling, the tacos can be wrapped in kitchen paper and foil.

VARIATION
Fill warm pitta breads with this spicy omelette mixture. Mini pitta breads are perfect for younger children who may find the folded tacos difficult to handle.

FRENCH COUNTRY-STYLE EGGS

THIS VARIATION ON AN OMELETTE COOKS THE "FILLING" IN THE OMELETTE MIXTURE ITSELF. YOU CAN INCORPORATE LOTS OF DIFFERENT INGREDIENTS, SUCH AS LEFTOVER VEGETABLES.

SERVES TWO

INGREDIENTS
45–75ml/3–5 tbsp sunflower oil
50g/2oz thick bacon rashers
    (strips) or pieces, rinds removed
    and chopped
2 thick slices of bread,
    cut into small cubes
1 small onion, chopped
1–2 celery sticks, thinly sliced
115g/4oz cooked potato, diced
5 eggs, beaten
2 garlic cloves, crushed
handful of young spinach or
    sorrel leaves, stalks removed,
    torn into pieces
few sprigs of parsley, chopped
salt and ground black pepper

1 Heat the oil in a large heavy-based frying pan, and fry the bacon and bread cubes until they are crisp and turning golden. Add the chopped onion, celery and diced potato, and continue cooking slowly, stirring frequently until all the vegetables are soft and beginning to turn golden brown.

2 Beat the eggs with the garlic and seasoning, and pour over the vegetables. When the underside is beginning to set, add the spinach or sorrel. Cook until they have wilted and the omelette is only just soft in the middle. Fold the omelette in half and slide it out of the pan. Serve topped with the parsley, if liked.

SPANISH OMELETTE

ALMOST REGARDED AS THE NATIONAL DISH OF SPAIN, THE TRADITIONAL SPANISH OMELETTE CONSISTS SIMPLY OF POTATOES, ONIONS AND EGGS. THIS ONE HAS OTHER VEGETABLES AND WHITE BEANS, TOO, A VARIATION FROM NORTHERN SPAIN, AND MAKES A VERY SUBSTANTIAL VEGETARIAN MEAL.

SERVES SIX

INGREDIENTS
   30ml/2 tbsp olive oil, plus extra
   1 Spanish (Bermuda) onion, chopped
   1 small red (bell) pepper, seeded
     and diced
   2 celery sticks, chopped
   225g/8oz potatoes, peeled, diced
     and cooked
   400g/14oz can cannellini
     beans, drained
   8 eggs
   salt and ground black pepper
   sprigs of oregano, to garnish
   green salad and olives, to serve

1 Heat the olive oil in a 30cm/12in frying pan or paella pan. Add the onion, red pepper and celery, and cook for 3–5 minutes until the vegetables are soft, but not coloured.

2 Add the potatoes and beans, and cook for several minutes to heat through.

3 In a small bowl, beat the eggs with a fork, then season well and pour over the ingredients in the pan.

4 Stir the egg mixture with a wooden spatula until it begins to thicken, then allow it to cook over a low heat for about 8 minutes. The omelette should be firm, but still moist in the middle. Cool slightly then invert on to a serving plate.

5 Cut the omelette into thick wedges. Serve warm or cool with a green salad and olives and a little olive oil. Garnish with oregano.

COOK'S TIP
In Spain, this omelette is often served as a tapas dish or appetizer. It is delicious served cold, cut into bite-size pieces and accompanied with a chilli sauce or mayonnaise for dipping. Other sliced seasonal vegetables, baby artichoke hearts and chick-peas can also be used in this recipe.

SPICY SAUSAGE AND CHEESE TORTILLA

A COLOURFUL, SPANISH-STYLE OMELETTE, WHICH IS DELICIOUS HOT OR COLD. CUT INTO WEDGES AND SERVE WITH A FRESH TOMATO AND BASIL SALAD.

SERVES FOUR TO SIX

INGREDIENTS
  75ml/5 tbsp olive oil
  175g/6oz chorizo or spicy sausages,
    thinly sliced
  675g/1½lb potatoes, peeled and
    thinly sliced
  275g/10oz onions, halved and
    thinly sliced
  4 eggs, beaten
  30ml/2 tbsp chopped fresh parsley,
    plus extra to garnish
  115g/4oz/1 cup Cheddar cheese, grated
  salt and ground black pepper

1 Heat 15ml/1 tbsp of the oil in a non-stick frying pan, about 20cm/8in in diameter, and fry the sausage until golden brown and cooked through. Lift out with a slotted spoon and drain on kitchen paper.

2 Add a further 30ml/2 tbsp oil to the pan and fry the potatoes and onions for 2–3 minutes, turning frequently (the pan will be very full). Cover tightly and cook over a gentle heat for about 30 minutes, turning occasionally, until softened and slightly golden.

3 In a mixing bowl, mix the beaten eggs with the parsley, cheese, sausage and plenty of seasoning. Gently stir in the potatoes and onions until well coated, taking care not to break up the potato slices too much.

4 Wipe out the pan with kitchen paper and heat the remaining 30ml/2 tbsp oil. Add the potato mixture and cook over a very low heat, until the egg begins to set. Use a palette knife to prevent the tortilla from sticking to the sides.

5 Preheat the grill to hot. When the base of the tortilla has set, which should take about 5 minutes, protect the pan handle with foil and place under the grill until the tortilla is set and golden. Cut into wedges and serve garnished with parsley.

FRITTATA WITH SUN-DRIED TOMATOES

A FRITTATA IS AN ITALIAN OMELETTE AND, LIKE A SPANISH OMELETTE, IT IS COOKED UNTIL FIRM
ENOUGH TO BE CUT INTO WEDGES AND CAN BE SERVED HOT, WARM OR COLD.

SERVES THREE TO FOUR

INGREDIENTS
6 sun-dried tomatoes
60ml/4 tbsp olive oil
1 small onion, finely chopped
pinch of fresh thyme leaves
6 eggs
50g/2oz/⅔ cup freshly grated
  Parmesan cheese
salt and ground black pepper
sprigs of thyme, to garnish
shavings of Parmesan, to serve

1 Place the tomatoes in a small bowl and pour on enough hot water to just cover them. Leave to soak for about 15 minutes. Lift the tomatoes out of the water and pat dry on kitchen paper. Reserve the soaking water. Cut the tomatoes into thin strips.

2 Heat the oil in a large non-stick frying pan. Stir in the chopped onion and cook for 5–6 minutes or until softened and golden. Stir in the sun-dried tomatoes and thyme, and cook over a moderate heat for a further 2–3 minutes, stirring from time to time. Season with salt and ground black pepper.

3 Break the eggs into a bowl and beat lightly. Stir in 45ml/3 tbsp of the tomato soaking water and the Parmesan. Raise the heat under the frying pan. When the oil is sizzling, add the eggs. Mix quickly into the other ingredients, then stop stirring. Lower the heat to moderate and cook for 4–5 minutes, or until the base is golden and the top puffed.

4 Take a large plate, place it upside down over the pan and, holding it firmly with oven gloves, turn the pan and the frittata over on to it. Slide the frittata back into the pan, and continue cooking for 3–4 minutes until golden brown on the second side. Remove from the heat. Cut the frittata into wedges, garnish with sprigs of thyme and serve.

STUFFED THAI OMELETTES

THAI FOOD OFTEN CLEVERLY COMBINES HOT CHILLI WITH SWEET FLAVOURS, AS IN THE FILLING FOR THE OMELETTES. IT MAKES AN INTERESTING CONTRAST TO THE DELICATE FLAVOUR OF THE EGG.

SERVES FOUR

INGREDIENTS
30ml/2 tbsp vegetable oil
2 garlic cloves, finely chopped
1 small onion, finely chopped
225g/8oz/2 cups minced (ground) pork
30ml/2 tbsp Thai fish sauce
5ml/1 tsp granulated (white) sugar
2 tomatoes, peeled and chopped
15ml/1 tbsp chopped fresh
  coriander (cilantro), and sprigs of
  coriander and red chillies, sliced,
  to garnish
ground black pepper
For the omelettes
5–6 eggs
15ml/1 tbsp Thai fish sauce
30ml/2 tbsp vegetable oil

1 Heat the oil in a wok, add the garlic and onion, and fry for 3–4 minutes until soft. Add the pork and fry for about 8 minutes until lightly browned.

2 Stir in the fish sauce, sugar, tomatoes and pepper; simmer until slightly thickened. Mix in the fresh coriander.

3 To make the omelettes, whisk together the eggs and fish sauce.

4 Heat 15ml/1 tbsp of the oil in an omelette pan or wok. Add half the beaten egg mixture and tilt the pan to spread the egg into a thin, even sheet.

5 Cook until the omelette is just set, then spoon half the filling into the centre. Fold into a neat square parcel by bringing the opposite sides of the omelette towards each other – first the top and bottom, then the right and left sides.

6 Slide the parcel on to a warm serving dish, folded side down. Repeat with the rest of the oil, eggs and filling to make a second omelette parcel. Garnish with sprigs of coriander and red chillies. Cut each omelette in half to serve.

COOK'S TIP
For a milder flavour, discard the seeds and membrane of the chillies where most of their heat resides. Always remember to wash your hands immediately after handling chillies.

OMELETTES FOO YUNG

THESE UNUSUAL BREAKFAST OMELETTES ARE SERVED WITH A TRADITIONAL CHINESE FILLING.

SERVES FOUR

INGREDIENTS
  15ml/1 tbsp groundnut (peanut) or
    vegetable oil
  40g/1½oz/3 tbsp spring onions
    (scallions), chopped
  2 celery sticks
  10ml/2 tsp minced fresh root ginger
  1 garlic clove, minced
  40g/1½oz/¼ cup diced cooked ham
  75g/3oz/½ cup crab meat
  75g/3oz/½ cup peeled cooked
    small prawns (shrimp)
  25ml/1½ tbsp chopped fresh
    coriander (cilantro)
  15–30ml/1–2 tbsp soy sauce,
    plus extra for serving
  8–12 eggs, beaten
  80g/3oz/6 tbsp butter
  salt and ground black pepper
  sprigs of coriander, to garnish

1 Heat the oil in a large frying pan over a medium heat. Add the spring onions, celery, ginger and garlic, and cook for about 1 minute, stirring frequently.

2 Add the ham, crab meat, prawns, fresh coriander and soy sauce. Reduce the heat and leave the mixture to gently heat through, stirring occasionally.

3 To make the omelettes, heat 20g/¾oz/ 1½ tbsp butter in a pan. Season the eggs, add a quarter of the mixture to the pan and cook until it begins to set. Turn over and cook for 2 minutes. Tip on to a serving plate and keep warm. Cook another 3 omelettes in the same way. Divide the filling between the omelettes and roll up. Serve hot with soy sauce and garnish with coriander.

EGG RICE CAKES WITH MUSHROOMS

THE CREAMY TASTE AND TEXTURE OF THESE RICE CAKES IS SET OFF BEAUTIFULLY BY THE EARTHY FLAVOUR OF THE WILD MUSHROOMS.

SERVES FOUR

INGREDIENTS
  1 egg
  15ml/1 tbsp plain (all-purpose) flour
  60ml/4 tbsp freshly grated Parmesan,
    Fontina or Pecorino cheese
  450g/1lb/2 cups cooked long
    grain rice
  50g/2oz/4 tbsp unsalted butter
  30–45ml/2–3 tbsp olive oil
  1 shallot or small onion, chopped
  175g/6oz/1¾ cups assorted wild and
    cultivated mushrooms, such as
    ceps, chanterelles, horn of plenty,
    blewits, field (portobello) and oyster
    mushrooms, trimmed and sliced
  sprig of thyme, plus extra to garnish
  30ml/2 tbsp sherry
  150ml/¼ pint/⅔ cup sour cream
    or crème fraîche
  salt and ground black pepper
  paprika, for dusting (optional)

1 Beat the egg, flour and cheese together with a fork, then stir in the cooked rice. Mix well and set aside.

2 Melt half the butter and oil in a frying pan and sauté the shallot or onion until soft but not brown. Add the mushrooms and thyme, and cook until the mushroom juices run. Stir in the sherry. Increase the heat to reduce the juices and concentrate the flavour. Season to taste. Remove from the heat and keep warm.

3 Heat the remaining butter and oil in a large frying pan and fry spoonfuls of the rice mixture in batches. Cook for about 1 minute, then turn over with a spatula and cook for a further 1 minute.

4 When all the rice cakes are cooked, arrange them on 1 large or 4 individual warmed plates, with the mushrooms and a spoonful of sour cream or crème fraîche. Garnish with a sprig of thyme. Dust with paprika if you wish.

SOUPS AND STARTERS

Both the cooking qualities of eggs and their decorative nature make them the ideal ingredient for tempting soups and starters. Eggs can be used to thicken soups, such as Egg and Cheese Soup and Saffron Fish Soup, and can be used as attractive garnishes in soups such as Cauliflower Cream Soup and Prawn and Egg-knot Soup.

Many cold starters, such as Asparagus and Egg Terrine, and Prawn, Egg and Avocado Mousses, rely on eggs for setting, and are ideal for dinner parties because they can be prepared in advance. Delicate starters, such as Quail's Eggs with Herbs, and Vegetable Tempura, will whet the appetite at the beginning of a meal, while more substantial starters, such as Twice-baked Soufflés and New Orleans Artichokes with Eggs, will please those with heartier appetites.

SAFFRON FISH SOUP

FILLING YET NOT TOO RICH, THIS GOLDEN SOUP WILL MAKE A DELICIOUS MEAL ON EARLY SUMMER EVENINGS, SERVED WITH LOTS OF HOT FRESH BREAD AND A GLASS OF FRUITY, DRY WHITE WINE. WHEN MUSSELS ARE NOT AVAILABLE USE PRAWNS IN THEIR SHELLS INSTEAD.

SERVES FOUR

INGREDIENTS

    1 parsnip, quartered
    2 carrots, quartered
    1 onion, quartered
    2 celery sticks, quartered
    2 smoked bacon rashers (strips),
      rinds removed
    juice of 1 lemon
    pinch of saffron threads
    450g/1lb fish heads
    450g/1lb live mussels, scrubbed
    1 leek, shredded
    2 shallots, finely chopped
    30ml/2 tbsp chopped dill, plus extra
      sprigs to garnish
    450g/1lb haddock, skinned and boned
    3 egg yolks
    30ml/2 tbsp double (heavy) cream
    salt and ground black pepper

1 Put the parsnip, carrots, onion, celery, bacon, lemon juice, saffron strands and fish heads in a large saucepan with 900ml/1½ pints/3¾ cups water and bring to the boil. Boil gently for about 20 minutes or until reduced by half.

COOK'S TIP
Fish stock freezes well and will keep for up to 6 months.

2 Discard any mussels that are open and don't close when tapped sharply. Add the rest to the pan of stock. Cook for about 4 minutes until they have opened. Strain the soup and return the liquid to the pan. Discard any unopened mussels, then remove the remaining ones from their shells and set aside.

3 Add the leeks and shallots to the soup, bring to the boil and cook for 5 minutes. Add the dill and haddock, and simmer for a further 5 minutes until the fish is tender. Remove the haddock, using a slotted spoon, then flake it into a bowl, using a fork.

4 In another bowl, whisk together the eggs and double cream. Whisk in a little of the hot soup, then whisk the mixture back into the hot but not boiling liquid. Continue to whisk for several minutes as it heats through and thickens slightly, but do not let it boil.

5 Add the flaked haddock and mussels to the soup and check the seasoning. Garnish with tiny sprigs of dill and serve piping hot.

EGG FLOWER SOUP

THIS SIMPLE, HEALTHY SOUP IS FLAVOURED WITH FRESH ROOT GINGER AND CHINESE FIVE-SPICE POWDER. IT IS QUICK AND DELICIOUS AND CAN BE MADE AT THE LAST MINUTE.

SERVES FOUR

INGREDIENTS
   1.2 litres/2 pints/5 cups fresh
   chicken or vegetable stock
   10ml/2 tsp peeled, grated fresh
   root ginger
   10ml/2 tsp light soy sauce
   5ml/1 tsp sesame oil
   5ml/1 tsp Chinese five-spice powder
   15–30ml/1–2 tbsp cornflour
   (cornstarch)
   2 eggs
   salt and ground black pepper
   1 spring onion (scallion), finely
   sliced diagonally and 15ml/1 tbsp
   chopped coriander (cilantro) or flat
   leaf parsley, to garnish

COOK'S TIP
This soup is a good way of using up
leftover frozen egg yolks or whites.

1 Put the chicken or vegetable stock
into a large saucepan with the ginger,
soy sauce, oil and five-spice powder.
Bring to the boil and allow to simmer
gently for about 10 minutes.

2 Blend the cornflour in a measuring
jug with 60–75ml/4–5 tbsp water and
stir into the stock. Cook, stirring
constantly, until slightly thickened.
Season to taste with salt and pepper.

3 In a jug, beat the eggs together with
30ml/2 tbsp cold water until the mixture
becomes frothy.

4 Bring the soup back just to the boil
and drizzle in the egg mixture, stirring
vigorously with chopsticks. Choose a jug
with a fine spout to form a very thin
drizzle. Serve at once, sprinkled with
the sliced spring onions and chopped
coriander or parsley.

CAULIFLOWER CREAM SOUP

THIS DELICATELY FLAVOURED, THICK WINTER SOUP IS ENRICHED AT THE LAST MINUTE WITH CHOPPED HARD-BOILED EGGS AND CRÈME FRAÎCHE.

SERVES FOUR

INGREDIENTS

1 cauliflower, cut into large pieces
1 large onion, roughly chopped
1 large garlic clove, chopped
bouquet garni
5ml/1 tsp ground coriander
pinch of mustard powder
900ml/1½ pints/3¾ cups vegetable
  or chicken stock
5–10ml/1–2 tsp cornflour (cornstarch)
150ml/¼ pint/⅔ cup milk
45ml/3 tbsp crème fraîche
2 eggs, hard-boiled and
  roughly chopped
15ml/1 tbsp chopped fresh
  coriander (cilantro)
salt and ground black pepper

VARIATION
Use one or two large heads of broccoli
in place of the cauliflower.

1 Place the cauliflower in a large pan with the onion, garlic, bouquet garni, coriander, mustard, salt and pepper and stock. Simmer for 10–15 minutes until the cauliflower is tender. Cool slightly.

2 Remove the garlic and bouquet garni, then blend the cauliflower and onion with some of the cooking liquid in a food processor, or press through a sieve (strainer) for a really smooth result. Return to the pan along with the rest of the liquid.

3 Blend the cornflour with a little of the milk, then add to the soup with the rest of the milk. Return to the heat and cook until thickened, stirring all the time. Season to taste and, just before serving, turn off the heat and blend in the crème fraîche. Stir in the chopped egg and coriander and serve at once.

COOK'S TIP
Garlic croûtons would make a delicious accompaniment to this smooth soup.

AVGOLEMONO

THE NAME OF THIS POPULAR GREEK SOUP MEANS "EGG AND LEMON", THE TWO KEY INGREDIENTS. IT IS A LIGHT, NOURISHING SOUP MADE WITH ORZO, A GREEK RICE-SHAPED PASTA, BUT YOU CAN USE ANY VERY SMALL PASTA SHAPE IN ITS PLACE.

SERVES FOUR TO SIX

INGREDIENTS

1.75 litres/3 pints/7½ cups
  chicken stock
115g/4oz/½ cup orzo pasta
3 eggs
juice of 1 large lemon
salt and ground black pepper
lemon slices, to garnish

COOK'S TIP
To make your own chicken stock, place a chicken carcass in a large pan with 1 onion, 1 carrot, 1 celery stick, 1 garlic clove and a bouquet garni, cover with water and bring to the boil. Simmer for 2 hours, skimming occasionally. Strain the stock and use as required.

1 Pour the stock into a large pan and bring to the boil. Add the pasta and cook for 5 minutes.

COOK'S TIP
Do not allow the soup to boil once the eggs have been added or they will curdle.

2 Beat the eggs until frothy, then add the lemon juice and 15ml/1 tbsp cold water.

3 Stir in a ladleful of the hot chicken stock, then add 1–2 more. Return this mixture to the pan, off the heat, and stir well. Season and serve at once, garnished with lemon slices.

PRAWN AND EGG-KNOT SOUP

OMELETTES AND PANCAKES ARE OFTEN USED TO ADD PROTEIN TO LIGHT ORIENTAL SOUPS. IN THIS RECIPE, THIN OMELETTES ARE TWISTED INTO LITTLE KNOTS AND ADDED AT THE LAST MINUTE.

SERVES FOUR

INGREDIENTS
  1 spring onion (scallion), shredded
  800ml/1⅓ pints/3½ cups well-
    flavoured stock or instant dashi
  5ml/1 tsp soy sauce
  dash of sake or dry white wine
  pinch of salt
For the prawn (shrimp) balls
  200g/7oz/generous 1 cup raw large
    prawns (shrimp), shelled
  65g/2½ oz cod fillet, skinned
  5ml/1 tsp egg white
  5ml/1 tsp sake or dry white wine,
    plus a dash extra
  22.5ml/4½ tsp cornflour (cornstarch)
    or potato flour
  2–3 drops soy sauce
  pinch of salt
For the omelette
  1 egg, beaten
  dash of mirin
  pinch of salt
  oil, for cooking

3 To make the omelette, mix the egg with the mirin and salt. Heat a little oil in a frying pan and pour in the egg mixture, coating the pan evenly. When the omelette has set, turn it over and cook for 30 seconds. Leave to cool.

4 Cut the omelette into strips and tie each in a knot. Heat the stock or dashi, then add the soy sauce, sake or wine and salt. Divide the prawn balls and egg-knots among 4 bowls and add the soup. Garnish with the spring onion.

1 To make the prawn balls, use a pin to remove the black vein running down the back of each prawn. Place the prawns, cod, egg white, sake or dry white wine, cornflour or potato flour, soy sauce and a pinch of salt in a food processor or blender and process to a thick, sticky paste. Shape the mixture into 4 balls, place in a steaming basket and steam over a saucepan of vigorously boiling water for about 10 minutes.

2 To make the garnish, soak the spring onion in iced water for about 5 minutes, until they curl, then drain.

EGG AND CHEESE SOUP

IN THIS CLASSIC ROMAN SOUP, EGGS AND CHEESE ARE BEATEN INTO HOT SOUP, PRODUCING THE SLIGHTLY SCRAMBLED TEXTURE THAT IS CHARACTERISTIC OF THIS DISH.

SERVES SIX

INGREDIENTS
- 3 eggs
- 45ml/3 tbsp fine semolina
- 90ml/6 tbsp freshly grated Parmesan cheese
- pinch of nutmeg
- 1.5 litres/2½ pints/6¼ cups cold meat or chicken stock
- salt and ground black pepper
- 12 rounds of country bread or ciabatta, to serve

COOK'S TIP
Once added to the hot soup, the egg will begin to cook and the soup will become less smooth. Try not to overcook the soup at this stage because it may cause the egg to curdle.

1 Beat the eggs in a bowl, then beat in the semolina and the cheese. Add the nutmeg and beat in 250ml/8fl oz/ 1 cup of the meat or chicken stock. Pour the mixture into a measuring jug.

2 Pour the remaining stock into a large saucepan and bring to a gentle simmer.

3 A few minutes before you are ready to serve the soup, whisk the egg mixture into the hot stock. Raise the heat slightly, and bring it barely to the boil. Season and cook for 3–4 minutes.

4 To serve, toast the rounds of country bread or ciabatta, place two in each soup plate and ladle on the hot soup. Serve immediately.

NEW ORLEANS ARTICHOKES WITH EGGS

THIS COMBINATION OF ARTICHOKES WITH A TANGY SPINACH FILLING AND POACHED EGGS IN HOLLANDAISE SAUCE ORIGINATED IN NEW ORLEANS JAZZLAND. THE DISH HAS A TOUCH OF DEEP-SOUTH HEAT, IN THE FORM OF TABASCO SAUCE FROM LOUISIANA.

SERVES FOUR

INGREDIENTS
4 large artichokes
500g/1¼lb spinach, washed
50g/2oz/4 tbsp butter
30ml/2 tbsp plain (all-purpose) flour
175ml/6fl oz/¾ cup milk
4 canned anchovy fillets, drained
  and mashed
Tabasco sauce
salt, ground black pepper and
  grated nutmeg
4 eggs
For the hollandaise sauce
30ml/2 tbsp white wine vinegar
4 black peppercorns
1 bay leaf
2 egg yolks, at room temperature
115g/4oz/½ cup butter, cubed, at
  room temperature
salt and ground black pepper

1 With a sharp knife, cut the stems from the artichokes, then cut the top half off each and scoop out the centre leaves and the hairy "choke". Set aside.

2 Put the spinach into a deep pan with just the water that clings to the leaves. Cover and cook until soft. Tip into a colander and, when it is cool, squeeze out the moisture and chop finely.

3 Bring a wide pan of salted water to the boil. Add the artichokes, cover and cook for about 30 minutes or until tender. Lift out with a slotted spoon on to warmed serving plates and keep warm. Reserve the cooking water.

4 To make the hollandaise sauce, boil the vinegar with 30ml/2 tbsp water, the peppercorns and the bay leaf in a small pan until the liquid is reduced to 15ml/1 tbsp. Leave to cool.

5 Cream the egg yolks with one cube of soft butter and a pinch of salt in a heatproof bowl. Strain on the vinegar mixture, set the bowl over a pan of boiling water and turn off the heat.

6 Whisk in the remaining butter, a cube at a time, adding each cube just as the previous cube has melted. Carry on whisking until the sauce is shiny and thick. Season and leave over the pan of water to keep warm.

COOK'S TIP
The flesh at the base of each artichoke leaf tastes delicious dipped in hollandaise sauce. You may want to serve each artichoke with a small dish of sauce on the side for dipping. An egg cup makes an ideal vessel for this.

7 Melt 50g/2oz/4 tbsp butter in a large saucepan, mix in the flour and stir for 1 minute over the heat until the mixture begins to froth and bubble. Remove from the heat and gradually pour in the milk, stirring constantly with a wooden spoon. Return the pan to the heat and continue stirring until the sauce has thickened and reaches simmering point.

8 Stir the mashed anchovies into the sauce and leave to simmer for about 5 minutes. Add the chopped spinach and return to simmering point. Season with salt and black pepper, nutmeg and Tabasco sauce. Keep warm.

9 Bring the saucepan of water used to cook the artichokes to a gentle simmer. Break the eggs into individual cups and slide 2 eggs at a time into the water. Poach for about 3 minutes until the white is set, lift out using a slotted spoon and drain on kitchen paper.

10 Fill the artichokes with the spinach mixture. Set a poached egg on top of each and spoon hollandaise sauce over the artichokes. Serve at once.

TWICE-BAKED SOUFFLÉS

THESE LITTLE SOUFFLÉS ARE SERVED UPSIDE-DOWN. THEY ARE REMARKABLY SIMPLE TO MAKE AND CAN BE PREPARED UP TO A DAY IN ADVANCE, THEN REHEATED IN THE SAUCE JUST BEFORE SERVING. THEY ARE PERFECT FOR EASY, STRESS-FREE ENTERTAINING.

SERVES SIX

INGREDIENTS
20g/¾ oz/1½ tbsp butter
30ml/2 tbsp plain (all-purpose) flour
150ml/¼ pint/⅔ cup milk
1 small bay leaf
2 eggs, separated, plus 1 egg white
115g/4oz/1 cup Gruyère cheese, grated
1.5ml/¼ tsp cream of tartar
250ml/8fl oz/1 cup double
    (heavy) cream
25g/1oz/¼ cup flaked (sliced) almonds
salt, ground black pepper and
    grated nutmeg
sprigs of parsley, to garnish

1 Preheat the oven to 190°C/375°F/
Gas 5. Lightly grease six 175ml/6fl oz/
¾ cup ramekins, then line the bases
with buttered greaseproof paper.

2 In a small pan, melt the butter over a
medium heat, stir in the flour and cook
for 1 minute, stirring. Whisk in half the
milk until smooth, then whisk in the
remaining milk. Add the bay leaf and
seasoning. Bring to the boil and cook,
stirring constantly, for 1 minute.

3 Remove the pan from the heat and
discard the bay leaf. Beat the egg yolks,
one at a time, into the hot sauce, then
stir in the cheese until it is completely
melted. Set aside.

4 In a large, clean, grease-free bowl,
whisk the egg whites slowly until they
become frothy. Add the cream of tartar,
then increase the speed and whisk until
they form soft peaks that just flop over
at the top.

5 Whisk a spoonful of beaten egg whites
into the cheese sauce to lighten it. Pour
the cheese sauce over the remaining
whites. Using a rubber spatula or large
metal spoon, gently fold the sauce into
the whites, cutting down through the
centre to the bottom, then along the
side of the bowl and up to the top.

VARIATION
Other strongly flavoured cheeses could be
used in place of the Gruyère. Try mature
(sharp) Cheddar, blue Stilton, Emmental
or farmhouse Lancashire cheese.

6 Spoon the soufflé mixture into the
prepared ramekins, filling them about
three-quarters full. Put the ramekins in a
shallow baking dish and pour in boiling
water to come halfway up the sides of
the ramekins. Bake for about 18 minutes
until puffed and golden brown. Let the
soufflés cool in the ramekins just long
enough for them to deflate.

7 Increase the oven temperature to
220°C/425°F/Gas 7. Run a knife around
the edge of the soufflés and invert on to
an ovenproof dish or individual dishes.
Remove the lining paper.

8 Lightly season the cream and pour
over the soufflés, sprinkle with almonds
and bake for 10–15 minutes until well
risen and golden. Serve immediately,
garnished with sprigs of parsley.

COOK'S TIP
If you are making these soufflés in
advance, cool the once-cooked soufflés,
then cover and chill. It is important to
bring the soufflés back to room
temperature before baking, so remove
them from the fridge in plenty of time.

BAKED EGGS <u>WITH</u> CREAMY LEEKS

THIS SIMPLE BUT ELEGANT STARTER CAN ALSO BE MADE WITH OTHER VEGETABLES SUCH AS SPINACH PURÉE OR RATATOUILLE. IT IS PERFECT FOR LAST-MINUTE ENTERTAINING OR QUICK DINING.

SERVES FOUR

INGREDIENTS
15g/½oz/1 tbsp butter, plus extra
  for greasing
225g/8oz small leeks, thinly sliced
75–90ml/5–6 tbsp whipping cream
freshly grated nutmeg
4 small–medium eggs
a few sage leaves
sunflower oil
salt and ground black pepper

VARIATION
For a slightly different result, beat the eggs with the remaining cream and seasoning in step 4 and spoon over the leeks. Bake as normal.

1 Preheat the oven to 190°C/375°F/ Gas 5. Generously butter the base and sides of four ramekins.

2 Melt the butter in a frying pan and cook the leeks for 3–5 minutes over a medium heat, stirring frequently, until softened but not browned.

3 Add 45ml/3 tbsp of the cream and cook over a gentle heat for 5 minutes until the leeks are very soft and the cream has thickened a little. Season with salt, pepper and nutmeg.

4 Place the ramekins in a small roasting tin and divide the leeks among them. Break an egg into each, spoon over the remaining cream, and season.

5 Pour boiling water into the tin to come about halfway up the sides of the dishes. Transfer the tin to the oven and bake for about 10 minutes, until just set.

6 While the eggs are baking, fry the sage leaves in a little oil until crisp and scatter over the top of the eggs to serve.

VEGETABLE TEMPURA

TEMPURA ARE JAPANESE SAVOURY FRITTERS. THEY ARE TRADITIONALLY MADE WITH PRAWNS, BUT MONKFISH AND VEGETABLES CAN ALSO BE USED. THE SECRET OF MAKING THE INCREDIBLY LIGHT BATTER IS TO USE REALLY COLD WATER, AND TO HAVE THE OIL FOR FRYING AT THE RIGHT TEMPERATURE.

SERVES FOUR

INGREDIENTS

2 courgettes (zucchini)
½ aubergine (eggplant)
1 large carrot
½ small Spanish (Bermuda) onion
1 egg
120ml/4fl oz/½ cup iced water
115g/4oz/1 cup plain
 (all-purpose) flour
vegetable oil, for deep frying
salt and ground black pepper
sea salt, lemon slices and Japanese
 soy sauce (shoyu), to serve

1 Using a potato peeler, pare strips of peel from the courgettes and aubergine to give a striped effect.

2 Using a chef's knife, cut the courgettes, aubergine and carrot into strips about 7.5–10cm/3–4in long and 6mm/¼in wide.

3 Put the courgettes, aubergine and carrot strips into a colander and sprinkle liberally with salt. Put a small plate over the vegetables, weight it down and leave for about 30 minutes, then rinse thoroughly under cold running water. Drain thoroughly, then dry the vegetables with kitchen paper.

4 Thinly slice the onion from top to base, discarding the plump pieces in the middle. Separate the layers so that there are lots of fine, long strips. Mix all the vegetables together and season with salt and pepper.

5 Make the batter immediately before frying. Mix the egg and iced water in a bowl, then sift in the flour. Mix briefly with a fork or chopsticks. Do not overmix; the batter should remain lumpy. Add the vegetables to the batter and mix to coat.

VARIATION
Other suitable vegetables for tempura include mushrooms and peppers.

6 Half-fill a wok with oil and heat to 180°C/350°F. Scoop up 1 heaped tablespoon of the mixture at a time and carefully lower it into the oil. Deep fry in batches for about 3 minutes until golden brown and crisp. Drain on kitchen paper.

7 Serve each portion with salt, slices of lemon and a tiny bowl of Japanese soy sauce for dipping.

STEAMED THAI EGGS WITH PRAWNS

THIS GENTLY COOKED EGG DISH CONTAINS A SURPRISING KICK OF CHILLI, GINGER AND GARLIC. BE SURE YOU HAVE A STEAMER, COLANDER OR SIEVE WITH A TIGHT-FITTING LID OTHERWISE THE EGGS WILL TAKE MUCH LONGER TO COOK.

SERVES FOUR

INGREDIENTS
  a little oil
  175g/6oz/1 cup peeled prawns (shrimp)
  5ml/1 tsp grated fresh root ginger
  5ml/1 tsp fish sauce
  1 large garlic clove, thinly sliced
  15–30ml/1–2 tbsp soy sauce
  2 large spring onions (scallions), sliced
  4 medium or small eggs
  50ml/2fl oz/¼ cup vegetable or
    chicken stock
  5ml/1 tsp sesame oil
  5ml/1 tsp very finely chopped fresh
    red chilli, plus extra to garnish
  salt and ground black pepper
  salad of finely shredded Chinese
    cabbage and thinly sliced
    cucumber, to serve (optional)

1 Lightly oil four large ramekin dishes. Put the prawns in a large bowl and stir in the ginger, fish sauce, garlic, soy sauce and half the spring onions.

COOK'S TIP
If the steamer does not have a tightly fitting lid, the eggs may need a little extra cooking time.

2 Put the eggs into another bowl, whisk in the stock, oil and chilli, without letting the eggs get too frothy. Add the prawn mixture and divide among the ramekins.

3 Place the ramekins in a steamer, over a pan of simmering water, cover and cook for 15 minutes until just set. Remove from the heat and leave to cool.

EGGS IN RED WINE

THIS IS A VARIATION ON A CLASSIC FRENCH RECIPE OEUFS EN MEURETTE BUT IS MUCH LIGHTER AND LESS RICH. TRADITIONALLY, THE EGGS ARE POACHED IN THE WINE RATHER THAN WATER.

SERVES SIX

INGREDIENTS
  40g/1½oz/3 tbsp butter
  150g/5oz streaky bacon, rinds
    removed, and roughly chopped
  1 large onion, chopped
  2 shallots, chopped
  1 large garlic clove, chopped
  750ml/1¼ pints/3 cups red wine
  1 clove
  5ml/1 tsp sugar
  1 bay leaf
  1 sprig fresh thyme or
    5ml/1 tsp dried
  25g/1oz/¼ cup plain
    (all-purpose) flour
  6 slices of French bread
  15g/½oz/1 tbsp butter, softened
  6 eggs
  salt and ground black pepper
  sprigs of thyme, to garnish

1 Melt half the butter in a pan and fry the bacon gently for 5 minutes. Then add the onion, shallots and garlic, and cook, stirring, for a further 5 minutes.

2 Add the wine, clove, sugar and herbs and simmer for about 15 minutes to reduce by about one-third.

3 Leave the sauce to cool until you can pick out the bacon to reserve. Remove the bay leaf, thyme and clove, then strain the sauce or purée in a blender.

4 Melt the rest of the butter in a pan and stir in the flour to make a roux. On a very low heat, gradually whisk in the wine purée and cook for 2–3 minutes until thickened, whisking all the time. Add 30–45ml/2–3 tbsp water to give a lighter consistency and whisk well. Return the bacon to the sauce.

5 Meanwhile, brush the bread on both sides with the soft or melted butter and grill until crisp and golden on both sides.

6 Break the eggs, two at a time, into cups and slide into a pan of simmering water. Poach for 3 minutes, then remove and drain on kitchen paper. To serve, spoon a little sauce on to the toast, top with the eggs and garnish with thyme.

MAIN MEALS

When you think of main meals, the first ingredient you think of isn't generally eggs. However, there are a number of delicious main dishes whose key ingredient is eggs. These dishes take advantage of the versatile qualities of eggs, either in their whole form or by combining them with other ingredients. Dishes such as Baked Cod with Hollandaise Sauce, and Spaghetti with Eggs, Bacon and Cream, rely on eggs for their rich and creamy sauces, while dishes such as Tomato Bread and Butter Pudding use eggs to bind them together. In contrast, dishes such as Egg and Lentil Curry, and Couscous with Eggs and Tomato Sauce, use whole boiled eggs to create delicious and tempting results.

SPAGHETTI WITH EGGS, BACON AND CREAM

THIS ITALIAN CLASSIC, FLAVOURED WITH PANCETTA AND A GARLIC AND EGG SAUCE THAT COOKS AROUND THE HOT SPAGHETTI, IS POPULAR WORLDWIDE. IT MAKES A GREAT LAST-MINUTE SUPPER.

3 Meanwhile, cook the spaghetti in a large saucepan of salted boiling water according to the instructions on the packet until *al dente*.

4 Put the eggs, crème fraîche and grated Parmesan in a bowl. Stir in plenty of black pepper, then beat together well.

5 Drain the pasta thoroughly, tip it into the pan with the pancetta or bacon and toss well to mix.

6 Turn off the heat under the pan, then immediately add the egg mixture and toss thoroughly so that it cooks lightly and coats the pasta.

7 Season to taste, then divide the spaghetti among 4 warmed bowls and sprinkle with freshly ground black pepper. Serve immediately, with extra grated Parmesan handed separately.

COOK'S TIP
You can replace the crème fraîche with either double (heavy) cream or sour cream, if you prefer.

SERVES FOUR

INGREDIENTS
30ml/2 tbsp olive oil
1 small onion, finely chopped
1 large garlic clove, crushed
8 pancetta or rindless smoked
   streaky bacon rashers (strips),
   cut into 1cm/½in strips
350g/12oz fresh or dried spaghetti
4 eggs
90–120ml/6–8 tbsp/½ cup
   crème fraîche
60ml/4 tbsp freshly grated
   Parmesan cheese, plus extra
   to serve
salt and ground black pepper

1 Heat the oil in a large saucepan, add the onion and garlic and fry gently for about 5 minutes until softened.

2 Add the pancetta or bacon to the pan and cook for 10 minutes, stirring.

BAKED COD <u>WITH</u> HOLLANDAISE SAUCE

SIMPLY COOKED FRESH FISH NEEDS LITTLE ASSISTANCE OTHER THAN A SPOONFUL OF CLASSIC HOLLANDAISE SAUCE. THIS RECIPE ALSO INCLUDES SOME VARIATIONS TO THE CLASSIC SAUCE.

SERVES FOUR

INGREDIENTS
    4 cod steaks or cutlets
    a little olive oil
    a squeeze of lemon juice
    15ml/1 tbsp fresh white breadcrumbs
    15ml/1 tbsp roughly ground hazelnuts
    salt and ground black pepper
    a few sprigs of dill, to garnish
    chips and mixed leaf salad, to serve
For the hollandaise sauce
    30ml/2 tbsp lemon juice
    2 egg yolks
    115g/4oz/½ cup butter, melted and
        cooled slightly

3 Whisk in the egg yolks, then, over a very gentle heat, add the butter in a slow stream, whisking all the time. Keep whisking until glossy and thick, then season to taste. Keep warm over a pan of hot water, until ready to serve.

4 Top the fish with the sauce and garnish with dill. Serve with chips and a mixed leaf salad.

VARIATIONS
To make anchovy sauce, whisk in 2–3 mashed anchovy fillets and keep whisking until they dissolve. Season after adding the anchovy. This sauce may only need pepper as anchovy fillets are very salty. To make herb sauce, whisk in 30ml/2 tbsp finely chopped fresh dill and leave to stand 5–10 minutes before serving for the flavour to come out. To make tomato hollandaise sauce, stir in 30ml/2 tbsp very finely chopped plum tomatoes and add extra pepper to taste.

1 Preheat the oven to 200ºC/400ºF/ Gas 6. Brush both sides of the cod with oil and lemon juice. Season, then mix together the crumbs, nuts and seasoning and press on to the fish. Place on a baking tray and bake for 15–20 minutes.

2 Meanwhile, prepare the hollandaise sauce. Simmer the lemon juice with 30ml/2 tbsp water in a small pan for a couple of minutes until reduced by at least half. Cool slightly.

SMOKED FISH SOUFFLÉ PUDDING

THIS SUPERB DISH IS AN INTERESTING CROSS BETWEEN A SOUFFLÉ AND A FISH PIE, SUBSTANTIAL
ENOUGH FOR A SUNDAY LUNCH OR A WINTER SUPPER. IT'S EASY TO EAT, SO CHILDREN WILL LOVE IT.

SERVES FOUR TO FIVE

INGREDIENTS
  450g/1lb smoked haddock or cod,
    soaked for 20 minutes in cold water
  350g/12oz cooked, peeled potatoes,
    kept warm
  50g/2oz/4 tbsp butter
  45ml/3 tbsp snipped fresh chives,
    plus extra to garnish
  3 eggs, separated
  15ml/1 tbsp lemon juice
  salt and ground black pepper

COOK'S TIP
For extra flavour, add a splash of dry
white vermouth or white wine to the fish
poaching water.

1 Preheat the oven to 180°C/350°F/
Gas 4. Drain the smoked haddock or
cod, place in a large pan, cover in cold
water and bring to simmering point.
Poach the fish for 5–7 minutes until it
flakes easily. Cool slightly, then drain
well and remove the skin and bones.

2 Mash the potatoes thoroughly with the
butter, chives, egg yolks and seasoning.
Stir in the flaked fish and lemon juice.
Whisk the egg whites until stiff and fold
in. Spoon into a buttered, deep
ovenproof dish and bake for 35 minutes
or until well risen and golden on top.

EGG AND GREEN VEGETABLE RISOTTO

THE ADDITION OF EGGS TURNS THIS ITALIAN FAVOURITE INTO A DELICATE, CREAMY DISH. SERVE IT
WITH CHUNKS OF COUNTRY BREAD OR A CRISP FENNEL AND RADICCHIO SALAD.

SERVES FOUR

INGREDIENTS
  50g/2oz/¼ cup butter
  1 onion, chopped
  2 garlic cloves, crushed
  225g/8oz/scant 1¼ cups Arborio
    or risotto rice
  600–750ml/1–1¼ pints/2½–3 cups
    good chicken or vegetable
    stock, hot
  3 eggs
  75g/3oz/1 cup freshly grated
    Parmesan cheese
  15ml/1 tbsp lemon juice
  115g/4oz spinach, green cabbage
    or chard, shredded
  salt and ground black pepper

VARIATION
For a country-style risotto, use sorrel
instead of spinach. Omit the lemon juice
because this vegetable already has a
slightly sharp flavour.

1 Melt the butter in a heavy-based
saucepan. Add the onion and garlic and
cook gently until softened, stirring
occasionally. Add the rice and stir until
thoroughly coated in butter, then pour
on 300ml/½ pint/1¼ cups of the stock.

COOK'S TIP
If you have leftover rice you can use it in
this dish. Omit step 2, then add the
eggs, cheese and lemon juice as above
and cook gently until soft and creamy.
Other green vegetables can be used
instead. Try cooked leeks or asparagus.

2 Over a gentle heat, slowly bring the
mixture to the boil, then simmer, stirring
only once, until the liquid is absorbed.
Add another 300ml/½ pint/1¼ cups of
stock and cook until all this liquid has
been absorbed.

3 Beat together the eggs, cheese,
lemon juice, green vegetable and
seasoning. Stir into the rice and cook
very gently for about 5 minutes, adding
more stock if the mixture seems too
stiff. The perfect risotto has a soft and
creamy texture.

BAKED HERB CRÊPES

TURN LIGHT HERB PANCAKES INTO SOMETHING SPECIAL. FILL WITH A SPINACH, CHEESE AND PINE NUT FILLING, THEN BAKE AND SERVE WITH A DELICIOUS TOMATO SAUCE.

SERVES FOUR

INGREDIENTS
25g/1oz/⅔ cup chopped fresh herbs
15ml/1 tbsp sunflower oil, plus extra
    for frying
120ml/4fl oz/½ cup milk
3 eggs
25g/1oz/¼ cup plain
    (all-purpose) flour
pinch of salt
For the sauce
30ml/2 tbsp olive oil
1 small onion, chopped
2 garlic cloves, crushed
400g/14oz can chopped tomatoes
pinch of soft light brown sugar
For the filling
450g/1lb cooked fresh spinach, drained
175g/6oz ricotta cheese
25g/1oz pine nuts, toasted
5 sun-dried tomato halves in olive
    oil, drained and chopped
30ml/2 tbsp shredded fresh basil
salt, nutmeg and ground black pepper
4 egg whites
oil, for greasing

1 To make the crêpes, place the herbs and oil in a food processor and blend until smooth. Add the milk, eggs, flour and salt and process again until smooth. Leave to rest for 30 minutes.

2 Heat a small non-stick frying pan and add a very small amount of oil. Pour out any excess oil and pour in a ladleful of the batter. Swirl around to cover the base. Cook for 2 minutes, turn over and cook for a further 1–2 minutes. Make the remaining 7 crêpes in the same way.

3 To make the sauce, heat the oil in a pan, add the onion and garlic and cook gently for 5 minutes. Add the tomatoes and sugar and cook for about 10 minutes until thickened. Purée in a blender, then sieve (strainer) and set aside.

4 To make the filling, mix together the spinach with the ricotta, pine nuts, tomatoes and basil. Season with salt, nutmeg and pepper.

5 Preheat the oven to 190°C/375°F/ Gas 5. Whisk the 4 egg whites until stiff. Fold one-third into the spinach mixture, then gently fold in the rest.

6 Place one crêpe at a time on a lightly oiled baking sheet, add a spoonful of filling and fold into quarters. Bake for 12 minutes until set. Reheat the sauce and serve with the crêpes.

SMOKED SALMON AND HERB ROULADE

A LITTLE SMOKED SALMON GOES A LONG WAY IN THE FILLING FOR THIS DELICATELY FLAVOURED ROULADE. MAKE THE ROULADE IN ADVANCE TO GIVE IT TIME TO COOL, BUT DON'T PUT IT IN THE FRIDGE OR IT WILL LOSE ITS LIGHT TEXTURE.

2 Prepare a 33 × 28cm/13 × 11in Swiss roll tin and preheat the oven to 180°C/ 350°F/Gas 4. Whisk the egg whites and fold into the yolk mixture, then pour into the tin and bake for 12–15 minutes. Leave, covered with greaseproof paper, for 10–15 minutes, then tip out on to greaseproof paper sprinkled with a little Parmesan. Allow to cool.

3 Mix together the crème fraîche, chopped smoked salmon, chopped dill and seasoning.

4 Spread over the roulade and roll up, then leave to firm up in a cold place. Sprinkle with the rest of the Parmesan and garnish with lamb's lettuce.

SERVES SIX TO EIGHT

INGREDIENTS
25g/1oz/2 tbsp butter
25g/1oz/¼ cup plain (all-purpose) flour
175ml/6fl oz/¾ cup milk, warm
3 large eggs, separated
50g/2oz/⅔ cup freshly grated
  Parmesan cheese
30ml/2 tbsp chopped fresh dill
30ml/2 tbsp chopped fresh parsley
150ml/¼ pint/⅔ cup full fat
  crème fraîche
115g/4oz smoked salmon,
  coarsely chopped
salt and ground black pepper
lamb's lettuce, to garnish

1 Melt the butter in a heavy-based pan, blend in the flour and cook over a low heat to a thick paste. Then gradually stir in the milk, whisking as it thickens, and cook for 1–2 minutes to make a thick sauce. Stir in the egg yolks, two-thirds of the Parmesan cheese, the herbs and salt and ground black pepper to taste.

COOK'S TIP
Roulades are ideal for entertaining because they can be made in advance. To ring the changes, use other strong-flavoured cheeses, or add cooked fresh salmon, tuna or prawns to the filling instead of Parmesan and smoked salmon.

SPICED MINCE WITH SOUFFLÉ TOPPING

YOU WILL FIND VERSIONS OF THIS DISH AROUND THE WORLD UNDER DIFFERENT NAMES. IN SOUTH AFRICA IT IS CALLED BOBOTEE, IN INDIA AND THE EAST IT IS KEEMA PER ENDA.

SERVES FOUR

INGREDIENTS

    30ml/2 tbsp vegetable oil or ghee
    2 onions, finely chopped
    2 large garlic cloves, crushed
    1cm/½in piece fresh root ginger,
      peeled and grated
    15ml/1 tbsp chilli powder
    10ml/2 tsp ground coriander
    5ml/1 tsp ground cumin
    15ml/1 tbsp ground turmeric
    675g/1½lb minced (ground) beef
      or lamb
    2 large tomatoes, chopped
    4 eggs
    10ml/2 tsp cornflour (cornstarch)
    30–45ml/2–3 tbsp chopped fresh
      coriander (cilantro) or parsley
    salt and ground black pepper
    rice, noodles or baked potatoes
      and a mixed salad, to serve

1 Heat the oil or ghee in a pan and sauté the onion and garlic until soft. Add the ginger and spices and fry for 2 minutes. Add the mince and stir over a high heat until browned.

2 Add 150ml/¼ pint/⅔ cup water and the tomatoes and simmer for about 12 minutes or until the liquid has reduced. Transfer to an ovenproof dish. Preheat the oven to 190°C/375°F/Gas 5.

3 Separate the egg yolks and whites and place in separate bowls. Whisk the yolks with the cornflour and seasoning. Stiffly whisk the egg whites, then fold in the yolks and half the coriander or parsley. Spoon the egg mixture over the mince and cook for 20 minutes or until well risen and golden. Sprinkle with the rest of the coriander or parsley. Serve piping hot with a mixed salad and rice, noodles or baked potatoes, if liked.

TOMATO BREAD AND BUTTER PUDDING

THIS IS A GREAT FAMILY DISH AND IS IDEAL WHEN YOU DON'T HAVE TIME TO COOK ON THE DAY BECAUSE IT CAN BE PREPARED IN ADVANCE. IT MAKES A WONDERFUL WARMING SUPPER.

SERVES FOUR

INGREDIENTS

    50g/2oz/4 tbsp butter, softened
    15ml/1 tbsp red pesto sauce
    1 garlic and herb foccacia
    2 large ripe tomatoes, sliced
    150g/5oz mozzarella cheese,
      thinly sliced
    300ml/½ pint/1¼ cups milk
    3 large eggs
    5ml/1 tsp fresh chopped oregano,
      plus extra to garnish
    50g/2oz Pecorino Romano or Fontina
      cheese, grated
    salt and ground black pepper

COOK'S TIP
If you like, you could use other cheeses such as Beaufort, Bel Paese or Taleggio, in this pudding.

1 Preheat the oven to 180°C/350°F/ Gas 4. Blend together the butter and pesto sauce in a small bowl. Slice the herb bread and spread one side of each slice with the pesto mixture.

2 In an oval ovenproof dish, layer the bread slices with the mozzarella and tomatoes, overlapping each new layer with the next.

3 Beat together the milk, eggs and oregano, season well and pour over the bread. Leave to stand for 5 minutes.

4 Sprinkle over the grated cheese and bake the pudding in the oven for about 40 minutes or until golden brown and just set. Serve immediately, straight from the dish, sprinkled with more coarsely chopped oregano.

SALADS AND SIDE DISHES

Eggs make the ideal addition to salads. They are delicious warm or cold and complement the fresh taste of classic recipes such as Salad Niçoise and Caesar Salad. Adding eggs to a salad can also turn it into the perfect light lunch or supper dish, try Warm Dressed Salad with Poached Eggs, and Egg and Fennel Tabbouleh with Nuts.

There are also a number of delicious side dishes that include eggs; try Baked Mediterranean Vegetables in their crispy egg-rich batter, Roasted Ratatouille Moussaka with its wonderfully light, egg topping and Florets Polonaise with its garnish of crumbled egg.

CAESAR SALAD

THIS MUCH-ENJOYED SALAD WAS CREATED BY CAESAR CORDONI IN TIJUANA IN 1924. BE SURE TO USE COS LETTUCE AND ADD THE SOFT EGGS AND GARLIC CROÛTONS AT THE LAST MINUTE.

3 Add the remaining olive oil to the salad leaves and season with salt and pepper. Toss to coat well.

4 Break the soft-boiled eggs on top. Sprinkle with the lemon juice and toss to combine the ingredients.

5 Add the grated Parmesan cheese and anchovies, if using, then toss again.

6 Scatter the croûtons on top of the salad and serve immediately.

COOK'S TIPS
To make a tangier dressing, mix the olive oil with 30ml/2 tbsp white wine vinegar, 2.5ml/½ tsp mustard, 5ml/1 tsp sugar, and salt and pepper.

SERVES SIX

INGREDIENTS
175ml/6fl oz/¾ cup salad oil, preferably olive oil
115g/4oz/2 cups French or Italian bread, cut in 2.5cm/1in cubes
1 large garlic clove, crushed with the flat side of a knife
1 cos or romaine lettuce
2 eggs, boiled for 1 minute
120ml/4fl oz/½ cup lemon juice
50g/2oz/⅔ cup freshly grated Parmesan cheese
6 anchovy fillets, drained and finely chopped (optional)
salt and ground black pepper

1 Heat 50ml/2fl oz/¼ cup of the oil in a frying pan. Add the bread and garlic and fry, stirring and turning constantly, until the cubes are golden brown. Drain on kitchen paper and discard the garlic.

2 Tear large lettuce leaves into smaller pieces. Put all the lettuce in a bowl.

SALAD NIÇOISE

MADE WITH THE FRESHEST OF INGREDIENTS, THIS CLASSIC PROVENÇAL SALAD MAKES A SIMPLE YET UNBEATABLE SUMMER DISH. SERVE WITH COUNTRY-STYLE BREAD AND CHILLED WHITE WINE.

SERVES FOUR

INGREDIENTS
 115g/4oz French (green) beans,
   trimmed and cut in half
 115g/4oz mixed salad leaves
 ½ small cucumber, thinly sliced
 4 ripe tomatoes, quartered
 50g/2oz can anchovies, drained and
   halved lengthways
 4 eggs, hard-boiled
 1 tuna steak, about 175g/6oz
 olive oil, for brushing
 ½ bunch small radishes, trimmed
 50g/2oz/½ cup small black olives
 salt and ground black pepper
For the dressing
 90ml/6 tbsp extra virgin olive oil
 2 garlic cloves, crushed
 15ml/1 tbsp white wine vinegar

4 Preheat the grill. Brush the tuna steak with olive oil and sprinkle with salt and black pepper. Grill for 3–4 minutes on each side until cooked through. Allow to cool, then flake with a fork.

5 Scatter the flaked tuna, anchovies, quartered eggs, radishes and olives over the salad. Pour over the dressing and toss together lightly to combine. Serve at once.

1 To make the dressing, whisk together the oil, garlic and vinegar and season to taste with salt and pepper. Set aside.

2 Cook the French beans in a saucepan of boiling water for 2 minutes until just tender, then drain.

3 Mix together the salad leaves, sliced cucumber, tomatoes and French beans in a large, shallow bowl. Halve the anchovies lengthways and shell and quarter the eggs.

VARIATION
Opinions vary on whether Salad Niçoise should include potatoes but, if you like, include a few small cooked new potatoes.

POTATOES WITH EGG AND LEMON DRESSING

THIS OLD-FASHIONED SALAD TAKES ON A NEW LEASE OF LIFE WHEN MIXED WITH HARD-BOILED EGGS AND LEMON JUICE. ITS TANGY FLAVOUR IS PERFECT TO ACCOMPANY A SUMMER BARBECUE.

SERVES FOUR

INGREDIENTS
900g/2lb new potatoes
1 small onion, finely chopped
2 eggs, hard-boiled
300ml/½ pint/1¼ cups mayonnaise
1 garlic clove, crushed
finely grated rind and juice of
  1 lemon
60ml/4 tbsp chopped fresh parsley,
  plus extra for garnishing
  (optional)
salt and ground black pepper

COOK'S TIP
For a health-conscious meal, choose a reduced-fat mayonnaise or, alternatively, replace the mayonnaise with low-fat Greek (US strained plain) yogurt and use the lemon juice from just half of the lemon.

1 Scrub or scrape the potatoes, cover with cold water and bring to the boil. Add salt and simmer for 15 minutes, or until tender. Drain and allow to cool. Cut the potatoes into large dice, season well and combine with the chopped onion.

2 Shell the hard-boiled eggs, set aside the yolk and roughly chop the whites. Place the whites in a mixing bowl and stir in the mayonnaise. Mix the garlic, lemon rind and lemon juice in a small bowl and stir them into the mayonnaise mixture, combining thoroughly.

3 Stir the mayonnaise mixture into the potatoes, coating them well, then fold in the chopped parsley. Press the egg yolk through a sieve (strainer) and sprinkle on top. Serve cold or chilled, garnished with parsley, if you like.

VARIATION
Replace the potato with cooked beetroot (beet). The mayonnaise will turn bright pink, which may surprise your guests, but the flavour is excellent. Alternatively, use a mixture of potatoes and beetroot.

SPRINGTIME SALAD WITH QUAIL'S EGGS

ENJOY SOME OF THE BEST EARLY SEASON GARDEN VEGETABLES IN THIS CRUNCHY GREEN SALAD. IT IS MADE WITH TINY QUAIL'S EGGS AND THE CONTRAST OF FRESH FLAVOURS IS DELIGHTFUL.

SERVES FOUR

INGREDIENTS
175g/6oz broad (fava) beans
175g/6oz fresh peas
175g/6oz asparagus
175g/6oz very small new
  potatoes, scrubbed
8 quail's eggs, soft-boiled
  and peeled
45ml/3 tbsp good lemon
  mayonnaise
45ml/3 tbsp sour cream or
  crème fraîche
½ bunch mint, chopped, with
  a few whole leaves reserved
  for garnishing
salt and ground black pepper

1 Cook the broad beans, peas, asparagus and new potatoes in separate pans of lightly salted boiling water until just tender.

2 Mix together the beans, peas, asparagus, potatoes and the eggs.

3 Blend together the mayonnaise, sour cream or crème fraîche and chopped mint in a jug (pitcher) and add seasoning to taste. Pour the dressing over the salad and toss gently adding the whole mint leaves at the last minute. Serve immediately.

SALAD WITH OMELETTE STRIPS AND BACON

RICH DUCK EGGS ARE DELICIOUS IN SALADS AND, WHEN COOKED AS AN OMELETTE, THEY HAVE A LOVELY, DELICATE FLAVOUR.

SERVES FOUR

INGREDIENTS
    400g/14oz bag of mixed salad leaves
    6 streaky bacon rashers (strips),
        rinds removed and chopped
    2 duck eggs
    2 spring onions (scallions), chopped
    few sprigs of coriander
        (cilantro), chopped
    25g/1oz/2 tbsp butter
    60ml/4 tbsp olive oil
    30ml/2 tbsp balsamic vinegar
    salt and ground black pepper

COOK'S TIP
Choose a selection of salad leaves, which includes distinctive flavours that will add a bite to this salad. A combination that includes rocket (arugula), watercress or herbs would be ideal.

1 Warm an omelette pan over a low heat and gently fry the chopped bacon until the fat runs. Increase the heat to crisp up the bacon, stirring frequently. When the bacon pieces are brown and crispy, remove from the heat and transfer to a hot dish to keep warm.

2 Beat the eggs with the spring onions and coriander and season.

3 Melt the butter in an omelette pan and pour in the beaten eggs. Cook for 2–3 minutes to make an unfolded omelette. Cut into long strips and add to the salad with the bacon.

4 Place the salad leaves in a large bowl. Add the oil, vinegar and seasoning to the omelette pan, heat briefly and pour over the salad. Toss well before serving.

CHILLI SALAD OMELETTES WITH HUMMUS

THESE DELICATE OMELETTES ARE FILLED WITH SALAD AND SERVED CHILLED, MAKING A REFRESHING LUNCH.

SERVES SIX

INGREDIENTS
    4 eggs
    15ml/1 tbsp cornflour (cornstarch)
    15ml/1 tbsp stock or water
    115g/4oz/1 cup shredded salad
        vegetables, such as crisp lettuce,
        carrot, celery, spring onions
        (scallions) and (bell) peppers
    60ml/4 tbsp chilli salad dressing
        (or add a few drops of chilli sauce
        to your favourite salad dressing)
    60–75ml/4–5 tbsp hummus
    4 crisply cooked bacon rashers
        (strips), chopped
    salt and ground black pepper

VARIATIONS
These omelettes can be filled with a whole range of ingredients. Try using taramasalata instead of hummus, or fill the omelettes with ratatouille.

1 Break the eggs into a bowl. Add the cornflour and stock or water and beat well. Heat a lightly oiled frying pan and pour a quarter of the egg mixture into the pan, tipping it to spread it out to a thin, even layer. Cook the omelette gently to avoid it colouring too much or becoming bubbly and crisp. When cooked, remove from the pan and make a further 3 omelettes in the same way. Stack them between sheets of greaseproof paper, then cool and chill.

2 When ready to serve, toss the shredded salad vegetables together with 45ml/3 tbsp of the dressing. Spread half of each omelette with hummus, top with the salad vegetables and chopped bacon and fold in half. Drizzle the rest of the dressing over the filled omelettes before serving.

COOK'S TIP
These wafer-thin omelettes can be made well in advance and stored in the fridge.

ROASTED RATATOUILLE MOUSSAKA

Based on the classic Greek dish, this moussaka really has a taste of the Mediterranean. Roasting brings out the deep rich flavours of the vegetables, which give a colourful contrast to the light and mouthwatering egg-and-cheese topping. This dish is perfect as a hearty winter side dish or as a vegetarian main course.

SERVES FOUR TO SIX

INGREDIENTS
  2 red (bell) peppers, seeded and cut
    into large chunks
  2 yellow (bell) peppers, seeded and
    cut into large chunks
  2 aubergines (eggplants), cut into
    large chunks
  3 courgettes (zucchini), thickly sliced
  45ml/3 tbsp olive oil
  3 garlic cloves, crushed
  400g/14oz can chopped tomatoes
  30ml/2 tbsp sun-dried tomato paste
  45ml/3 tbsp chopped fresh basil or
    15ml/1 tbsp dried basil
  15ml/1 tbsp balsamic vinegar
  1.5ml/¼ tsp soft light brown sugar
  salt and ground black pepper
  basil leaves, to garnish
For the topping
  25g/1oz/2 tbsp butter
  25g/1oz/¼ cup plain
    (all-purpose) flour
  300ml/½ pint/1¼ cups milk
  1.5ml/¼ tsp freshly grated nutmeg
  250g/9oz ricotta cheese
  3 eggs, beaten
  25g/1oz/⅓ cup freshly grated
    Parmesan cheese

1 Preheat the oven to 230°C/450°F/ Gas 8. Arrange the peppers, aubergines and courgettes in an even layer in a large roasting tin. Season well with salt and ground black pepper.

2 Mix together the oil and crushed garlic cloves and pour them over the vegetables. Shake the roasting tin to thoroughly coat the vegetables in the garlic mixture.

3 Roast in the oven for 15–20 minutes until slightly charred, lightly tossing the vegetables once during cooking time. Remove the tin from the oven and set aside. Reduce the oven temperature to 200°C/400°F/Gas 6.

4 Put the chopped tomatoes, sun-dried tomato paste, basil, balsamic vinegar and brown sugar in a large, heavy-based pan and heat to boiling point. Reduce the heat and simmer, uncovered, for 10–15 minutes until thickened, stirring occasionally. Season with salt and freshly ground black pepper to taste.

5 Carefully tip the roasted vegetables out of their tin and into the pan of tomato sauce. Mix well, coating the vegetables thoroughly in the tomato sauce. Spoon into an ovenproof dish.

6 To make the topping, melt the butter in a large, heavy-based pan over a gentle heat. Stir in the flour and cook for 1 minute. Pour in the milk, stirring constantly, then whisk until blended. Add the nutmeg and continue whisking over a gentle heat until thickened. Cook for a further 2 minutes, then remove from the heat and allow to cool slightly.

7 Mix in the ricotta cheese and beaten eggs thoroughly. Season with salt and plenty of freshly ground black pepper to taste.

8 Level the surface of the roasted vegetable mixture with the back of a spoon. Spoon the moussaka topping over the vegetables and sprinkle with the Parmesan cheese. Bake for 30–35 minutes until the topping is golden brown. Serve immediately, garnished with basil leaves.

VARIATION
Rather than baking this recipe in one large dish, divide the roasted vegetables and topping among individual gratin dishes. Reduce the baking time to 25 minutes. Individual portions can also be frozen and, when needed, simply removed from the freezer, allowed to thaw and baked for 30–35 minutes – ideal for those with a vegetarian in the family, or for unexpected guests.

CARROT AND PARSNIP GRATIN

CARROTS AND PARSNIPS BOTH CONTAIN NATURAL SUGARS, SO THIS GRATIN IS DELICIOUSLY SWEET-TASTING AND SUCCULENT. IT IS PERFECT FOR SERVING WITH MEATS SUCH AS PORK AND TURKEY, WHICH ARE TRADITIONALLY SERVED WITH SWEET ACCOMPANIMENTS, SUCH AS APPLE OR CRANBERRY SAUCE.

SERVES FOUR

INGREDIENTS
25g/1oz/2 tbsp butter, plus extra
  for greasing
1 large onion, halved and sliced
1 garlic clove, crushed
350g/12oz carrots, grated
350g/12oz parsnips, grated
2 eggs, beaten
150ml/¼ pint/⅔ cup single
  (light) cream
freshly grated nutmeg
25g/1oz/½ cup soft white
  breadcrumbs
salt and ground black pepper

COOK'S TIP
If you can, use organic vegetables for this recipe. As well as being healthier, organic vegetables can save you time as they do not need to be peeled and can simply be scrubbed and grated.

1 Preheat the oven to 180°C/350°F/ Gas 4. Heat the butter in a large frying pan or pan until it melts. Add the sliced onion and crushed garlic and cook gently until tender and transparent. Mix in the grated carrots and parsnips, cook for a few minutes, then season with plenty of salt and ground black pepper.

2 Butter a shallow, ovenproof dish and spoon the vegetable mixture into it, smoothing down the top with the back of the spoon.

3 In a large jug, beat the eggs with the cream, nutmeg and seasoning. Pour the egg mixture over the cooked grated vegetables and sprinkle with the breadcrumbs. Place the dish in the oven and bake for about 30 minutes until the gratin is firm to the touch and turning golden brown.

VARIATION
Try cooking other mixtures of root vegetables in this way, such as carrot and swede or celeriac and parsnip.

FLORETS POLONAISE

SIMPLE BOILED OR STEAMED VEGETABLES QUICKLY BECOME SOMETHING VERY SPECIAL WITH THIS PRETTY EGG TOPPING. THEY MAKE A PERFECT DINNER PARTY SIDE-DISH OR ARE GREAT WITH A WEEKDAY SUPPER.

SERVES SIX

INGREDIENTS
500g/1¼lb mixed vegetables, such as
  cauliflower, broccoli, romanesco
  and calabrese
50g/2oz/4 tbsp butter
finely grated rind of ½ lemon
1 large garlic clove, crushed
25g/1oz white breadcrumbs, lightly
  baked or grilled (broiled) until crisp
2 eggs, hard-boiled
salt and ground black pepper

VARIATIONS
Use toasted nuts instead of the crumbs if you wish and omit the garlic if you think guests may not like it.

1 Trim the vegetables and break into equal-size florets. Place the florets in a steamer over a pan of boiling water and steam for 12 minutes, or boil in salted water for 5–7 minutes, until just tender. Drain and toss in butter. Transfer to a heated serving dish.

2 While the vegetables are cooking, mix together the lemon rind, crushed garlic and grilled breadcrumbs. Finely chop the eggs and mix together with the remaining ingredients. Sprinkle the chopped egg mixture over the cooked vegetables and serve at once.

ASPARAGUS WITH EGG AND LEMON SAUCE

EGGS AND LEMONS ARE OFTEN FOUND IN DISHES FROM GREECE, TURKEY AND THE MIDDLE EAST. THIS SAUCE HAS A TANGY, FRESH TASTE AND BRINGS OUT THE BEST IN ASPARAGUS.

SERVES FOUR

INGREDIENTS

675g/1½lb asparagus, tough ends
  removed, and tied in a bundle
15ml/1 tbsp cornflour (cornstarch)
10ml/2 tsp sugar
2 egg yolks
juice of 1½ lemons
salt

VARIATIONS
This sauce goes very well with all sorts of young vegetables. Try it with baby leeks, cooked whole or chopped, or serve it with other baby vegetables, such as carrots and courgettes (zucchini).

1 Cook the bundle of asparagus in boiling salted water for 7–10 minutes.

2 Drain well and arrange the asparagus in a serving dish. Reserve 200ml/7fl oz/ scant 1 cup of the cooking liquid.

3 Blend the cornflour with the cooled, reserved cooking liquid and place in a small pan. Bring to the boil, stirring all the time, and cook over a gentle heat until the sauce thickens slightly. Stir in the sugar, then remove the pan from the heat and allow to cool slightly.

4 Beat the egg yolks thoroughly with the lemon juice and stir gradually into the cooled sauce. Cook over a very low heat, stirring all the time, until the sauce is fairly thick. Be careful not to overheat the sauce or it may curdle. As soon as the sauce has thickened, remove the pan from the heat and continue stirring for 1 minute. Taste and add salt or sugar as necessary. Allow the sauce to cool slightly.

5 Stir the cooled sauce, then pour a little over the asparagus. Cover and chill for at least 2 hours before serving with the rest of the sauce.

COOK'S TIP
Use tiny asparagus spears for an elegant starter or a special dinner party.

SPECIAL FRIED RICE

MORE COLOURFUL AND ELABORATE THAN OTHER FRIED RICE DISHES, SPECIAL FRIED RICE IS ALMOST A MEAL IN ITSELF AND IS IDEAL FOR A MIDWEEK SUPPER.

SERVES FOUR

INGREDIENTS

50g/2oz/⅓ cup cooked peeled
  prawns (shrimp)
3 eggs
5ml/1 tsp salt
2 spring onions (scallions), chopped
60ml/4 tbsp vegetable oil
115g/4oz lean pork, finely diced
15ml/1 tbsp light soy sauce
15ml/1 tbsp Chinese rice wine
450g/1lb/6 cups cooked rice
115g/4oz green peas

COOK'S TIP
The weight of rice increases about two
and a half times after cooking. When a
recipe calls for cooked rice, use just
under half the weight in uncooked rice.

1 Pat dry the prawns with kitchen
paper. Beat the eggs with a pinch of the
salt and a few pieces of spring onion.

2 Heat half the oil in a wok, add the
pork and stir-fry until golden. Add the
prawns and cook for 1 minute, then add
the soy sauce and rice wine or sherry.
Remove from the heat and keep warm.

3 Heat the remaining oil in the wok and
lightly scramble the eggs. Add the rice
and stir with chopsticks to make sure
that each grain of rice is separated.

4 Add the remaining salt and spring
onions, the stir-fried prawns, pork and
peas. Toss well over the heat to
combine and serve either hot or cold.

PASTRIES

Eggs are an essential ingredient in many pastry dishes. Not only are they used to make classic doughs, such as rich shortcrust pastry and choux pastry, they can also add a wonderful creamy richness to savoury fillings. Quiche Lorraine, and Leek and Onion Tartlets have rich egg fillings, which hold together the other key ingredients, while pastries, such as Mushroom and Quail's Eggs Gougère, and Egg and Salmon Puff Parcels contain whole boiled eggs within the pastry crust. Another interesting way of using eggs in pastries is to add a whole raw egg, which cooks as the pastry cooks. Fiorentina Pizza and Tuna Galette have eggs broken on top of them before baking, whereas the raw egg added to Tunisian Brik cooks inside the filo crust when the pastry is deep fried.

QUICHE LORRAINE

*THIS CLASSIC QUICHE FROM EASTERN FRANCE HAS SOME DELIGHTFUL, TRADITIONAL CHARACTERISTICS
THAT ARE OFTEN FORGOTTEN IN MODERN RECIPES, NAMELY VERY THIN PASTRY, A REALLY CREAMY AND
LIGHT, EGG-RICH FILLING, AND SMOKED BACON.*

SERVES FOUR TO SIX

INGREDIENTS

175g/6oz/1½ cups plain (all-purpose)
    flour, sifted
pinch of salt
115g/4oz/½ cup unsalted butter,
    at room temperature, diced
3 eggs, plus 3 yolks
6 smoked streaky bacon rashers
    (strips), rinds removed
300ml/½ pint/1¼ cups double
    (heavy) cream
25g/1oz/2 tbsp unsalted butter
salt and ground black pepper

1 Blend the flour, salt, butter and 1 egg
yolk in a food processor. Turn out on to
a floured surface and form the mixture
into a ball. Leave for 20 minutes.

2 Lightly flour a deep 20cm/8in round
flan tin, and place it on a baking tray.
Roll out the pastry and use to line the
tin, trimming off any overhanging
pieces. Gently press the pastry into the
corners of the tin. If the pastry breaks
up, don't worry, just gently push it into
shape. Chill for 20 minutes. Preheat
the oven to 200°C/400°F/Gas 6.

3 Meanwhile, cut the bacon into thin
strips and grill until the fat runs.
Arrange the bacon in the pastry case.
Beat together the cream, the remaining
eggs and yolks and seasoning, and pour
into the pastry case.

4 Bake for 15 minutes, then reduce the
heat to 180°C/350°F/Gas 4 and bake for
a further 15–20 minutes. When the
filling is puffed up and golden brown
and the pastry edge crisp, remove from
the oven and top with knobs of butter.
Stand for 5 minutes before serving.

COOK'S TIP

To prepare the quiche in advance, bake
for 5–10 minutes less than recommended,
until the filling is just set. Reheat later at
190°C/375°F/Gas 5 for about 10 minutes.

TUNA AND EGG GALETTE

THIS FLAKY PASTRY TART COMBINES SOFT-CENTRED EGGS AND A SLIGHTLY PIQUANT FISH FILLING. IT MAKES A WONDERFUL DISH FOR A SUMMER SUPPER AND IS ALSO A GREAT BUFFET-TABLE STANDBY.

SERVES FOUR

INGREDIENTS
2 sheets of ready-rolled puff pastry
flour, for rolling and egg, to glaze
60ml/4 tbsp olive oil
175g/6oz tuna steak
2 onions, sliced
1 red (bell) pepper, seeded
  and chopped
2 garlic cloves, crushed
45ml/3 tbsp capers, drained
5ml/1 tsp grated lemon rind
30ml/2 tbsp lemon juice
5 eggs
salt and ground black pepper
30ml/2 tbsp chopped flat leaf
  parsley, to garnish

1 Preheat the oven to 190°C/375°F/ Gas 5. Lay one sheet of pastry on a lightly floured baking tray and cut to a 28 × 18cm/11 × 7in rectangle. Brush the whole sheet with beaten egg.

2 Cut the second sheet of pastry to the same size. Cut out a rectangle from the centre and discard, leaving a 2.5cm/1in border. Carefully lift the border on to the first sheet. Brush the border with beaten egg and prick the base.

3 Bake the pastry case for about 15 minutes until golden and well risen.

COOK'S TIP
If you are using fresh, unfrozen pastry, the remaining rectangle of pastry can be wrapped in clear film and frozen. Allow to defrost at room temperature for one hour before using.

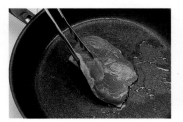

4 Heat 30ml/2 tbsp of the oil in a frying pan and fry the tuna steak for 2–3 minutes on each side until golden but still pale pink in the middle. Transfer to a plate and flake into small pieces.

5 Add the remaining oil to the pan and fry the onions, red pepper and garlic for 6–8 minutes until softened, stirring occasionally. Remove the pan from the heat and stir in the tuna, capers and lemon rind and juice. Season well.

6 Spoon the filling into the pastry case and level the surface with the back of a spoon. Break the eggs into the filling and return the galette to the oven for about 10 minutes, or until the eggs have just cooked through. Garnish with chopped parsley and serve at once.

COOK'S TIP
To make sure the eggs do not become hard on top during baking, cover the tart with lightly oiled foil.

CHEESE AND ONION FLAN

THE USE OF YEAST DOUGHS FOR TARTS AND FLANS IS POPULAR IN VARIOUS REGIONS OF FRANCE.
CHOOSE A STRONG CHEESE SUCH AS LIVAROT, MUNSTER OR PORT SALUT IN THIS RECIPE.

SERVES FOUR

INGREDIENTS

15g/½oz/1 tbsp butter
1 onion, halved and sliced
2 eggs
250ml/8fl oz/1 cup single
(light) cream
225g/8oz strong semi-soft cheese,
rind removed, sliced
salt and ground black pepper
salad leaves, to serve
For the yeast dough
10ml/2 tsp dried yeast
120ml/4fl oz/½ cup milk
5ml/1 tsp sugar
1 egg yolk
225g/8oz/2 cups plain (all-purpose)
flour, plus more for kneading
2.5ml/½ tsp salt
50g/2oz/4 tbsp butter, softened

1 To make the dough, place the yeast in a bowl. Warm the milk in a small saucepan until it is at body temperature and stir into the yeast with the sugar. Continue stirring until the yeast has dissolved completely. Leave the yeast mixture to stand for about 3 minutes, then beat in the egg yolk.

COOK'S TIP
If you prefer to use easy-blend yeast, omit step 1. Beat the egg yolk and milk together in a jug. Add the dry yeast to the flour and salt in the food processor, and pulse to combine. Pour in the egg and milk mixture, and proceed with the recipe as normal.

2 Put the flour and salt in a food processor fitted with a metal blade, and pulse to combine. With the machine running, slowly pour in the yeast mixture. Scrape down the sides and continue processing for 2–3 minutes. Add the softened butter and process for another 30 seconds.

3 Transfer the dough to a lightly greased bowl. Cover the bowl with a dish towel and allow to rise in a warm place for about 1 hour until the dough has doubled in bulk.

4 Remove the dough from the bowl and place on a lightly floured surface. Knock back the dough by punching down on it. Sprinkle a little more flour on the work surface and roll out the dough to a 30cm/12in round.

5 Line a 23cm/9in flan tin or dish with the dough. Gently press it into the tin or dish and trim off any overhanging pieces, leaving a 3mm/⅛in rim around the flan case. Cover with a dish towel, set aside in a warm place and leave the dough to rise again for about 30 minutes, or until puffy.

6 Meanwhile, melt the butter in a heavy-based saucepan and add the onion. Cover the pan and cook over a medium-low heat for about 15 minutes, until softened, stirring occasionally. Remove the lid and continue cooking, stirring frequently, until the onion is very soft and caramelized.

7 Preheat the oven to 180°C/350°F/ Gas 4. Beat together the eggs and cream. Season and stir in the cooked onion.

8 Arrange the cheese on the base of the flan case. Pour over the egg mixture and bake for 30–35 minutes until the base is golden and the centre is just set. Cool slightly on a wire rack and serve warm with salad leaves.

HERBED GREEK PIES

IF YOU CAN, USE LARGE MUFFIN TINS TO MAKE THESE LITTLE PIES. THEY PROVIDE A DEEP CASE TO HOLD PLENTY OF THE DELICIOUSLY TANGY YOGURT FILLING.

MAKES EIGHT

INGREDIENTS
175g/6oz shortcrust pastry
45–60ml/3–4 tbsp tapenade or
  sun-dried tomato paste
1 large egg
100g/3¾oz/scant ½ cup thick Greek
  (US strained plain) yogurt
90ml/6 tbsp milk
1 garlic clove, crushed
30ml/2 tbsp chopped mixed herbs,
  such as thyme, marjoram, basil
  and parsley
salt and ground black pepper

COOK'S TIP
You can make mini tartlets from this
recipe, which are ideal for parties. Bake
for only 15 minutes with the filling.

1 Preheat the oven to 190°C/375°F/
Gas 5. Roll out the pastry thinly and cut
out eight rounds using a 7.5cm/3in
cutter. Line deep patty or muffin tins
with the pastry rounds, then line each
one with a small piece of greaseproof
paper. Bake for 15 minutes. Remove
the paper and cook for a further 5
minutes or until the cases are crisp.

2 Spread a little tapenade or tomato
paste in the base of each pastry case.
Whisk together the egg, yogurt, milk,
garlic, herbs and seasoning. Spoon
carefully into the pastry cases and bake
for 25–30 minutes or until the filling is
just firm and the pastry golden. Allow
the pies to cool slightly before carefully
removing from the tins and serving.

TOMATO AND BLACK OLIVE TART

THIS DELICIOUS TART HAS A FRESH, RICH MEDITERRANEAN FLAVOUR AND IS PERFECT FOR PICNICS, BUT IT CAN, OF COURSE, BE MADE ALL YEAR ROUND. IF YOU ARE TAKING THIS TART ON A PICNIC, USE A RECTANGULAR TIN FOR EASIER TRANSPORTING AND PORTIONING.

SERVES EIGHT

INGREDIENTS
375g/13oz shortcrust pastry, at
  room temperature
3 eggs, beaten
300ml/½ pint/1¼ cups milk
30ml/2 tbsp chopped fresh herbs,
  such as parsley, marjoram or basil
6 firm plum tomatoes
75g/3oz ripe Brie cheese
about 16 black olives, stoned
salt and ground black pepper

VARIATIONS
This tart is delicious made with other
cheeses. Try slices of Gorgonzola or
Camembert for a slightly stronger flavour
or, alternatively, scatter a few strips of
anchovy fillet over the tart before baking.

1 Preheat the oven to 190°C/375°F/
Gas 5. Roll out the pastry thinly on a
lightly floured surface. Line a 28 × 18cm/
11 × 7in loose-based rectangular flan
tin, trimming off any overhanging edges.

2 Line the pastry case with greaseproof
paper and baking beans, and bake blind
for 15 minutes. Remove the greaseproof
paper and beans and bake for a further
5 minutes until the base is crisp.

3 Meanwhile, mix together the eggs,
milk, seasoning and herbs. Slice the
tomatoes, cube the cheese, and slice
the olives. Place the prepared flan case
on a baking tray, arrange the tomatoes,
cheese and olives in the bottom of the
case, then pour in the egg mixture.
Transfer carefully to the oven and bake
for about 40 minutes until just firm and
turning golden. Slice hot or cool in the
tin, then serve.

LEEK AND ONION TARTLETS

THESE ATTRACTIVE LITTLE TARTLETS MAKE A WONDERFUL STARTER AND ARE PERFECT FOR BUFFETS. SMALLER VERSIONS CAN ALSO BE MADE AND MAKE WONDERFUL PARTY FOOD.

SERVES SIX

INGREDIENTS
  25g/1oz/2 tbsp butter, plus extra
  1 onion, thinly sliced
  2.5ml/½ tsp dried thyme
  450g/1lb/4 cups leeks, thinly sliced
  50g/2oz/½ cup Gruyère cheese, grated
  3 eggs
  300ml/½ pint/1¼ cups single
    (light) cream
  pinch of freshly grated nutmeg
  salt and ground black pepper
  mixed salad leaves, to serve
For the pastry
  175g/6oz/1½ cups plain
    (all-purpose) flour
  75g/3oz/6 tbsp cold butter
  1 egg yolk
  30–45ml/2–3 tbsp cold water
  2.5ml/½ tsp salt

1 For the pastry, sift the flour into a bowl and add the butter. Rub the butter into the flour until the mixture resembles fine breadcrumbs.

2 Make a well in the flour mixture. Beat together the egg yolk, water and salt. Pour into the well and mix lightly to form a stiff dough. Form into a flattened ball. Wrap and chill for 30 minutes.

3 Butter six 10cm/4in tartlet tins. On a lightly floured surface, roll out the dough until 3mm/⅛in thick then, using a 12.5cm/5in cutter, cut as many rounds as possible. Ease the rounds into the tins, pressing the pastry firmly into the base and sides. Reroll the trimmings and line the remaining tins. Prick the bases and chill for 30 minutes.

4 Preheat the oven to 190°C/375°F/Gas 5. Line the pastry cases with foil and fill with baking beans. Place them on a baking sheet and bake for 6–8 minutes until golden at the edges. Remove the foil and beans, and bake for 2 minutes until the bases appear dry. Transfer to a wire rack to cool. Reduce the oven temperature to 180°C/350°F/Gas 4.

5 In a large frying pan, melt the butter over a medium heat, then add the onion and thyme, and cook for 3–5 minutes until the onion is just softened, stirring frequently. Add the leeks and cook for 10–12 minutes until they are soft and tender. Divide the mixture among the pastry cases and sprinkle each with cheese, dividing it evenly.

6 In a medium bowl, beat the eggs, cream, nutmeg and salt and pepper. Place the pastry cases on a baking sheet and pour on the egg mixture. Bake for 15–20 minutes until set and golden. Transfer the tartlets to a wire rack to cool slightly, then remove them from the tins and serve warm or at room temperature with salad leaves.

EGG AND SALMON PUFF PARCELS

THESE ELEGANT PARCELS HIDE A MOUTH-WATERING COLLECTION OF FLAVOURS, AND MAKE A DELICIOUS STARTER OR LUNCH DISH. SERVE WITH CURRY-FLAVOURED MAYONNAISE OR HOLLANDAISE SAUCE.

SERVES SIX

INGREDIENTS

75g/3oz/scant ½ cup long grain rice
300ml/½ pint/1¼ cups fish stock
350g/12oz tail piece of salmon
juice of ½ lemon
15ml/1 tbsp chopped fresh dill
15ml/1 tbsp chopped fresh parsley
10ml/2 tsp mild curry powder
6 small eggs, soft-boiled
  and cooled
425g/15oz flaky or puff pastry
1 small egg, beaten
salt and ground black pepper

1 Cook the rice in the fish stock according to the packet instructions, then drain and set aside to cool. Preheat the oven to 220°C/425°F/Gas 7.

2 Place the salmon in a large saucepan and cover with cold water. Gently heat until not quite simmering and cook for 8–10 minutes until it flakes easily. Lift the salmon out of the pan with a fish slice, and remove the bones and skin. Flake the fish into the rice, add the lemon juice, herbs, curry powder and seasoning, and mix well. Peel the eggs.

3 Roll out the pastry and cut into six 14–15cm/5½–6in squares. Brush the edges with the beaten egg. Place a spoonful of the rice mixture in the middle of each square, push an egg into the centre and top with a little more of the rice mixture. Pull over the pastry corners to the middle to form a square parcel, pressing the joins together firmly to seal.

4 Brush the parcels with more beaten egg, place on a baking sheet and bake for 20 minutes, then reduce the oven temperature to 190°C/375°F/Gas 5 and cook for a further 10 minutes or until golden and crisp underneath. Cool slightly before serving.

EGG AND SPINACH PIE

THIS PIE WAS ORIGINALLY COOKED FOR GREEK EASTER CELEBRATIONS. IT IS TRADITIONALLY MADE WITH 33 LAYERS OF FILO PASTRY, EACH ONE REPRESENTING A YEAR OF CHRIST'S LIFE. IT MAKES AN EXCELLENT PICNIC DISH AS IT CAN BE MADE IN ADVANCE AND TRAVELS WELL IN ITS COOKING TIN.

SERVES TEN TO TWELVE

INGREDIENTS
oil, for greasing
675g/1½lb fresh or frozen spinach,
    cooked and chopped
115g/4oz/½ cup butter, melted
1 bunch spring onions (scallions),
    finely chopped
30ml/2 tbsp fresh marjoram
    or oregano, chopped or 10ml/
    2 tsp dried
350g/12oz ricotta or curd cheese
45ml/3 tbsp grated Parmesan cheese
60ml/4 tbsp double (heavy)
    cream, whipped
5ml/1 tsp grated fresh nutmeg
450g/1lb filo pastry
2 egg whites, stiffly whisked
8 eggs, hard-boiled and peeled
salt and ground black pepper

1 Lightly grease a deep 20 × 25cm/ 8 × 10in roasting tin. Preheat the oven to 190°C/375°F/Gas 5.

2 Make sure the spinach is well cooked and thoroughly dried. Return it to the pan and cook gently, stirring until all the excess liquid has evaporated.

COOK'S TIP
This pie makes perfect picnic food. Partially cool it in the tin, then invert it on to a large board. Clean the tin and return the pie to the tin for easy transporting. You may find it easier to cut the pie into portions before going on your picnic.

3 Heat 30ml/2 tbsp butter in a large saucepan and fry the onions until softened. Stir in the spinach and herb, and season with salt and ground black pepper to taste. Mix until well blended and the spinach is quite soft and smooth.

4 Beat the ricotta or curd cheese with the Parmesan, cream, nutmeg and seasoning until really smooth.

5 Use just over half the sheets of filo pastry for the base: brush each sheet with melted butter, and layer neatly in the tin, allowing any excess pastry to hang over the edges. Filo pastry is very delicate so it you may find it simpler to cut very large sheets in half for easier handling. Keep the rest of the pastry covered with a damp cloth to prevent it from drying out.

VARIATION
For a pie with a slightly sharper, tangy taste, replace the soft cheese with the same weight of feta cheese. Crumble the cheese and mix with the cream, nutmeg and seasoning in step 4.

6 Whisk the egg whites, then fold into the cheese. Fold in the spinach until evenly mixed. Spoon half the mixture into the tin and arrange the eggs on top. Cover with the rest of the filling and fold over any excess pastry edges.

7 Brush the remaining sheets of pastry with butter and place over the top in an even layer. Brush with more butter, then bake for about 1 hour until the pastry is golden and the pie feels quite firm.

8 Allow the pie to cool slightly, then carefully invert it on to a clean surface, and serve warm or leave to cool completely and serve cold.

PARTY FOODS AND DRINKS

Beautifully presented and delicious-tasting food and drink are all that a
party needs to make it a success. This chapter provides a whole host of hot
and cold snacks and nibbles. Dishes, such as Tapenade and Quail's Eggs
and Eggs Mimosa, can be prepared ahead of time and will make a beautiful
centrepiece on any table. Hot party food, such as Stilton Croquettes and
Cheese Aigrettes, can be prepared ahead of time and only need a
little last-minute cooking. They are sure to impress your guests
and get them in the party mood. This chapter also includes a tempting
selection of unusual egg-based party drinks, such as Brandied Eggnog
and Old-fashioned Lemonade, as well as the classic morning-
after remedy, Prairie Oyster.

PARTY EGGS

HARD-BOILED EGGS MAKE PERFECT PARTY FOOD. GIVE THEM A
VARIETY OF FILLINGS AND GARNISHES FOR A STUNNING CENTREPIECE.

EACH VARIATION FILLS SIX EGGS

EGGS WITH CAVIAR
INGREDIENTS
    4 spring onions (scallions), trimmed
      and very finely sliced
    30ml/2 tbsp sour cream
    5ml/1 tsp lemon juice
    25g/1oz/2 tbsp caviar
    salt and ground black pepper
    lemon rind and caviar, to garnish

1 Mix all the ingredients with the egg
yolks, spoon back into the egg whites
and garnish with lemon rind and caviar.

NUTTY DEVILLED EGGS
INGREDIENTS
    40g/1½oz cooked ham, chopped
    4 walnut halves, very finely chopped
    15ml/1 tbsp Dijon mustard
    15ml/1 tbsp mayonnaise
    5ml/1 tsp white wine vinegar
    few large pinches of cayenne pepper
    salt and ground black pepper
    paprika and gherkins, to garnish

1 Mix together all the ingredients with
the egg yolks, spoon into the whites and
garnish with paprika and gherkin slices.

PRAWN AND CUCUMBER EGGS
INGREDIENTS
    75g/3oz/½ cup cooked peeled prawns
      (shrimp), reserving 12 for garnish
      and the rest chopped
    25g/1oz cucumber, peeled
      and diced
    5ml/1 tsp tomato sauce
    15ml/1 tbsp lemon mayonnaise
    salt and ground black pepper
    fennel sprigs, to garnish

1 Mix all the ingredients with the egg
yolks, spoon back into the egg whites
and garnish with prawns and fennel.

GARLIC AND GREEN PEPPERCORN EGGS
INGREDIENTS
    5ml/1 tsp garlic purée or 1 large
      garlic clove, crushed
    45ml/3 tbsp whipped cream
      or crème fraîche
    salt and ground black pepper
    2.5ml/½ tsp green peppercorns,
      crushed, to garnish

1 Mix the garlic, cream, egg yolks and
seasoning. Place in a piping bag and
pipe into the egg whites. Sprinkle with
a few crushed peppercorns.

EGG CANAPÉS

THESE ELEGANT PARTY PIECES TAKE A LITTLE TIME TO MAKE, BUT THEY CAN BE PREPARED IN ADVANCE WITH THE FINAL TOUCHES ADDED JUST BEFORE YOUR GUESTS ARRIVE.

EACH VARIATION MAKES 12

TRUFFLE CANAPÉS
INGREDIENTS
   225g/8oz rich shortcrust pastry
   2 eggs, beaten
   15g/½oz/1 tbsp butter
   5ml/1 tsp truffle oil or a few slices or
    gratings of fresh truffle
   salt and ground black pepper
   snipped chives, to garnish

1 Preheat the oven to 190°C/375°F/
Gas 5. Roll out the pastry very thinly on
a lightly floured work surface and use to
line 12 very small tartlet or muffin tins.

2 Line the base of each pastry case with
greaseproof paper and bake for about
10 minutes. Remove the paper and
bake for a further 5 minutes until the
pastry is crisp and golden.

3 Season the beaten eggs, then melt
the butter in a pan, pour in the eggs
and stir constantly over a gentle heat.
When the eggs are almost set, stir in
the truffle oil or fresh truffle. Spoon the
mixture into the pastry cases and top
with chives. Serve warm or cold.

PRAWN AND TOMATO CANAPÉS
INGREDIENTS
   225g/8oz rich shortcrust pastry
   2 tomatoes, skinned,
    seeded and chopped
   12 large cooked prawns (shrimp),
    shelled but tails left on
   60ml/4 tbsp hollandaise sauce
   salt and ground black pepper
   fennel or chervil sprigs, to garnish

1 Preheat the oven to 190°C/375°F/
Gas 5. Roll out the pastry very thinly on
a lightly floured work surface and use to
line 12 very small tartlet or muffin tins.

2 Line the base of each pastry case with
greaseproof paper and bake for about
10 minutes. Remove the paper and
bake for a further 5 minutes until crisp.

3 Place some chopped tomato in the
base of each pastry cases and season
with salt and freshly ground black
pepper. Top with the prawns and spoon
on some hollandaise sauce. Warm
through briefly in the oven and serve
garnished with fennel or chervil.

WATERCRESS AND AVOCADO CANAPÉS
INGREDIENTS
   3–4 slices dark rye bread
   1 small ripe avocado
   15ml/1 tbsp lemon juice
   45ml/3 tbsp mayonnaise
   ½ bunch watercress, chopped,
    reserving a few sprigs to garnish
   6 quail's eggs, hard-boiled

1 Cut the bread into 12 rounds, using a
plain or fluted biscuit cutter.

2 Cut the avocado in half, around the
stone. Peel one half, then slice and dip
each piece in lemon juice. Place one
piece of avocado on each bread round.

3 Scoop the remaining avocado into a
bowl and mash. Mix in the mayonnaise
and watercress. Spoon a little of the
mixture on to each canapé, top with a
peeled, halved quail's egg and garnish
with a sprig of watercress.

SALMON AND CORIANDER CANAPÉS
INGREDIENTS
   3–4 slices dark rye bread
   2 eggs, hard-boiled and thinly sliced
   115g/4oz poached salmon
   coriander (cilantro) leaves, to garnish
For the lime and coriander mayonnaise
   45–60ml/3–4 tbsp mayonnaise
   5ml/1 tsp chopped fresh coriander
   5ml/1 tsp lime juice
   salt and ground black pepper

1 Cut the rye bread into 12 triangular
pieces, using a sharp knife.

2 Make the lime and coriander
mayonnaise. In a small bowl, mix
together the mayonnaise, chopped
coriander and lime juice in a small
bowl. Season with salt and freshly
ground black pepper to taste.

3 Top each bread triangle with a slice of
egg, a small portion of salmon and a
teaspoon of mayonnaise. Garnish with a
coriander leaf. Chill until ready to serve.

ROLLED OMELETTE

JAPANESE FOOD IS ALWAYS PREPARED AND SERVED WITH PRECISION AND ELEGANCE. THIS FIRMLY SET, ROLLED OMELETTE IS CUT INTO NEAT PIECES, SHOWING THE EXQUISITE LAYERING INSIDE. THE TEXTURE SHOULD BE SMOOTH AND SOFT, NOT LEATHERY, AND THE FLAVOUR IS SWEET-SAVOURY. MOOLI AND SOY SAUCE ARE PERFECT CONDIMENTS TO COMPLEMENT ITS FLAVOUR AND TEXTURE.

SERVES FOUR

INGREDIENTS
    8 eggs
    60ml/4 tbsp sugar
    20ml/4 tsp soy sauce
    90ml/6 tbsp sake or dry
      white wine
    vegetable oil, for cooking
    soy sauce or plum sauce, to serve
For the garnish
    8cm/3¼in piece of mooli
      (daikon), finely grated
    shiso leaves (optional)

1 Break the eggs into a large bowl, mix them together, using a pair of chopsticks and a cutting action.

2 In a small bowl, mix together the sugar with the soy sauce and sake or dry white wine. Lightly stir this mixture into the beaten eggs. Divide the mixture between 2 bowls so that it can be cooked in two equal batches.

3 Heat a little oil in a medium-size frying pan and carefully wipe out the excess with kitchen paper.

COOK'S TIPS
Japanese ginger pickles can be found in chiller compartments in good supermarkets or in specialist food stores. They have a refreshing, zesty flavour, which complements this omelette perfectly.

4 Pour a quarter of the mixture from one bowl into the frying pan, tilting it to coat the base in a thin layer. When the edge has set, but the middle is still moist, roll up the egg towards you.

5 Moisten a piece of kitchen paper with oil and grease the empty side of the pan. Pour in a third of the remaining egg mixture and lift up the rolled egg with your chopsticks to let the raw egg run underneath.

6 When the edges have set, roll up the omelette in the opposite direction, tilting the pan away from you so that the omelette rolls easily.

7 Slide the roll towards you again, grease the pan, using the oily kitchen paper. Pour half of the remaining egg mixture into the pan, lifting the egg roll and allowing the uncooked egg to run under it as before.

8 When set, insert the chopsticks in the side of the rolled omelette and flip it over towards the opposite side of the frying pan. Add the remaining egg and cook in the same way. Slide the roll so that the join is underneath. Cook for a further 10 seconds.

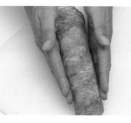

9 Slide the roll out on to a bamboo mat, if you have one, and roll up tightly, then press neatly into a rectangular shape. If you don't have a bamboo mat, simply press the omelette into a rectangle using your hands. Leave to cool.

10 Cook the remaining batch of egg mixture in the same way to make a second omelette roll. Slice the cold omelettes into 2.5cm/1in thick pieces, garnish with mooli and shiso leaves. Serve with soy or plum sauce.

EGGS MIMOSA

THE USE OF THE WORD MIMOSA DESCRIBES THE FINE YELLOW AND WHITE GRATED EGG, WHICH LOOKS VERY SIMILAR TO THE FLOWER OF THE SAME NAME. THIS PRETTY GARNISH CAN BE USED TO FINISH ANY DISH AND ADDS A LIGHT, SUMMERY TOUCH.

MAKES TWENTY-FOUR

INGREDIENTS
    12 eggs, hard-boiled and peeled
    2 ripe avocados, halved and stoned
    1 garlic clove, crushed
    a few drops of Tabasco sauce
    15ml/1 tbsp extra virgin olive oil
    salt and ground black pepper
    basil leaves, to garnish

COOK'S TIP
You can prepare the mimosa garnish in advance, but store the egg white and yolk separately, in small airtight containers, and keep them chilled.

1 Reserve 2 of the hard-boiled eggs and halve the remaining ones. Carefully remove the yolks with a teaspoon and blend together with the avocados, garlic, Tabasco sauce, oil and seasoning. Pipe or spoon the mixture into the halved egg whites.

2 Sieve (strain) the remaining egg whites and sprinkle over the filled eggs. Sieve the yolks on top. Arrange the filled egg halves on a serving platter. Sprinkle a little ground black pepper over the eggs and scatter with basil leaves to garnish, then serve.

CHEESE-CRUSTED PARTY EGGS

SIMILAR TO THE POPULAR SCOTCH EGG, THESE WHOLE SMALL EGGS ARE WRAPPED IN A DELICIOUS VEGETARIAN COATING THEN DEEP FRIED. THEY KEEP WELL FOR SEVERAL DAYS AND MAKE VERY GOOD PARTY SNACKS. THEY ARE ALSO IDEAL AS PICNIC AND TRAVEL FOOD.

MAKES SIX

INGREDIENTS
    115g/4oz/1⅔ cups stale
        white breadcrumbs
    ½ small leek, very finely chopped
    115g/4oz mild but tasty
        cheese, grated
    5ml/1 tsp garlic and herb seasoning
    30ml/2 tbsp chopped fresh parsley
    5ml/1 tsp mild mustard
    2 eggs, separated
    30–45ml/2–3 tbsp milk
    6 small spinach or sorrel leaves,
        stalks removed
    6 very small eggs, such as bantam,
        guinea fowl, or 8–10 quail's eggs,
        hard-boiled and peeled
    25–40g/1–1½oz/¼–⅓ cup flour,
        for coating, plus extra for dusting
    25g/1oz/2 tbsp sesame seeds,
        for coating
    oil, for deep frying
    salt and ground black pepper
    mayonnaise, to serve

1 Mix together the breadcrumbs, leeks, cheese, seasoning, parsley and mustard. Beat together the egg yolks and milk and blend into the mixture. Whisk 1 egg white until quite stiff and gradually work sufficient stiff egg white into the breadcrumb mixture to give a firm, dropping consistency. Chill for 1 hour.

COOK'S TIP
Make sure that you coat the eggs evenly first with the egg whites and then with the sesame flour to seal them completely before frying.

2 Divide the mixture into six portions. Mould one portion in the palm of your hand, place a spinach leaf inside and then an egg and carefully shape the mixture around the eggs to enclose them completely within a thin crust. Seal well and dust lightly with flour.

3 Beat the remaining egg white with 15ml/1 tbsp water, then pour into a shallow dish. Mix the flour with salt and pepper and the sesame seeds and place in another shallow dish. Dip the eggs first in the beaten egg white, then in the sesame flour. Cover and chill for at least 20 minutes.

4 Heat the oil in a saucepan until a crust of bread turns golden in about 1¼ minutes. Deep fry the eggs in the hot oil, turning frequently, until golden brown all over. Remove with a draining spoon, drain on kitchen paper and leave to cool. Serve, sliced in half, with a bowl of good mayonnaise for dipping.

PARMESAN THINS

THESE MELT-IN-THE-MOUTH BISCUITS ARE VERY MORE-ISH, SO MAKE PLENTY. DON'T JUST KEEP THEM FOR PARTIES — THEY MAKE A GREAT SNACK AT ANY TIME OF THE DAY.

MAKES SIXTEEN TO TWENTY

INGREDIENTS
50g/2oz/½ cup plain
  (all-purpose) flour
40g/1½oz/3 tbsp butter, softened
1 egg yolk
40g/1½oz/⅔ cup grated Parmesan
pinch each of salt and
  mustard powder

COOK'S TIP
If you want to make large quantities of these biscuits, freeze the dough in logs, wrapped in foil or clear film. To defrost, remove from the freezer and leave for at least 1 hour before cutting and baking.

1 Rub together the flour and the butter in a bowl, then work in the egg yolk, the cheese, salt and mustard. Mix to bring the dough together into a ball. Shape into a log, then wrap in foil or clear film and chill for at least 10 minutes.

2 Preheat the oven to 200°C/400°F/ Gas 6. Cut the dough log into very thin slices, about 3–6mm/⅛–¼in, and arrange on a baking tray. Flatten with a fork to give a pretty ridged pattern. Bake for 10 minutes or until crisp. Cool on a wire rack.

ELEGANT EGG SANDWICHES

A WELL-MADE EGG SANDWICH IS ONE OF THE BEST AND QUICKEST TEA-TIME SNACKS. HERE ARE TWO FAVOURITE FILLINGS, DELICIOUS AT ANY TIME OF DAY.

SERVES SIX

INGREDIENTS
  12 thin slices white or brown
    bread, crusts removed
  50g/2oz/4 tbsp butter, at
    room temperature
  slices of lemon, to garnish
For the egg and cress filling
  2 small hard-boiled eggs,
    chopped finely
  30ml/2 tbsp home-made
    mayonnaise
  ½ punnet mustard and cress
  salt and ground black pepper
For the egg and tuna filling
  2 small hard-boiled eggs, peeled
    and finely chopped
  25g/1oz canned tuna in oil, drained
    and mashed
  5ml/1 tsp paprika
  squeeze of lemon juice
  25g/1oz piece cucumber, peeled
    and thinly sliced

2 To make the egg and cress filling, mix the chopped eggs with the mayonnaise, cress and seasoning. Layer between six slices of bread. Press down gently and cut into neat triangles.

COOK'S TIP
These sandwiches will keep well for 2–3 hours. Cover with damp kitchen paper, then cover tightly in clear film. Chill until required.

3 To make the egg and tuna filling, mix the chopped eggs with the tuna, paprika, lemon juice and seasoning. Put cucumber on three slices of bread, top with the tuna mixture and the rest of the bread. Press down lightly and cut each sandwich into three neat fingers.

4 Arrange all the sandwiches on a plate and garnish with lemon slices.

1 Carefully trim the crusts off the bread, using a sharp knife, then spread the bread thinly with soft butter.

VARIATION
For harlequin sandwiches, use a combination of white and brown bread. Use a slice of brown bread for one side of each sandwich and a slice of white for the other. Arrange them on a plate, turning the sandwiches to show alternate brown and white sides.

BANANA AND MAPLE FLIP

THIS NOURISHING AND HEALTHY BREAKFAST DRINK IS PACKED WITH SO MUCH GOODNESS THAT YOU WON'T NEED ANYTHING ELSE FOR YOUR MORNING MEAL. AS IT IS MADE WITH A RAW EGG, DO BE SURE TO USE A REALLY FRESH FREE-RANGE ONE.

SERVES ONE

INGREDIENTS
    1 small banana, peeled and halved
    50g/2oz/¼ cup Greek (US strained
      plain) yogurt
    1 egg
    30ml/2 tbsp maple syrup
    5ml/1 tsp lemon juice
    2 ice cubes
    slice of orange, to serve (optional)

COOK'S TIPS
• To chill the glass quickly, place it in the freezer while you are preparing the drink.
• If your food processor isn't a heavy-duty model, crush the ice cubes first.

1 Put the banana, yogurt, egg, maple syrup, lemon juice and the ice cubes into a food processor or blender.

2 Blend continuously for 2 minutes until the mixture becomes really pale and frothy.

3 Pour into a tall, chilled glass and top with a slice of orange, if you like.

VARIATION
For a different fruity flavour, substitute a small, very ripe, peeled, stoned and chopped mango for the banana.

PRAIRIE OYSTER

BASED ON THE ORIGINAL MORNING-AFTER DRINK, WHICH IS TRADITIONALLY SERVED WITH A LARGE MEASURE OF SPIRITS, THIS IS A NON-ALCOHOLIC VERSION, ALTHOUGH YOU CAN ALWAYS ADD A SMALL SPLASH OF BRANDY IF YOU REALLY FEEL THE NEED. THE DRINK CONTAINS A RAW EGG YOLK SO DO BE SURE TO USE A FRESH ONE (SEE WATCHPOINT, BELOW).

SERVES ONE

INGREDIENTS
    5ml/1 tsp Worcestershire
      sauce
    5ml/1 tsp white wine vinegar
    5ml/1 tsp tomato ketchup
      or tomato sauce
    1 egg yolk, unbroken
    cayenne pepper

WATCHPOINT
The very young, the elderly, pregnant women and those in ill-health or with a compromised immune system are advised against consuming raw eggs or dishes and drinks containing raw eggs. This is because salmonella bacteria, which can cause severe food poisoning, are sometimes found in eggs and poultry. The bacteria are destroyed when eggs are heated to a temperature of 60°C/125°F.

1 Place the Worcestershire sauce, white wine vinegar and tomato ketchup or tomato sauce in a tall, narrow glass and mix together, using a long-handled spoon or stirrer.

2 Carefully slide the unbroken egg yolk into the glass but do not stir. Sprinkle in a little cayenne pepper and down the whole lot in one gulp.

COOK'S TIP
If you don't like the idea of swallowing a whole raw egg yolk, try whizzing together all the ingredients in a food processor or blender with some freshly squeezed orange juice.

COLD
DESSERTS

Many of our classic cold desserts depend on eggs for their rich, creamy or light textures. Whisked egg whites create the crisp, yet chewy, texture of pavlova, while the same whisked egg whites also create the light and creamy delight of Cold Lemon Soufflé with Almonds. Combining light egg whites with egg yolks can also produce the divinely rich Bitter Chocolate Mousses and Chocolate Chestnut Roulade. Many cold desserts use a classic egg custard as their base. Banana with Apricot Caramel Trifle is layered with thick fresh custard, while in Custard Tart with Plums the custard is cooked with fruit inside a crisp pastry shell. Classic baked custards include Baked Custard with Burnt Sugar and Baked Caramel Custard.

BAKED CUSTARD WITH BURNT SUGAR

THIS PUDDING IS THOUGHT TO HAVE ORIGINATED IN ENGLAND IN THE 18TH CENTURY AND HAS STOOD THE TEST OF TIME WELL. THE SOFT AND CREAMY EGG CUSTARD IS FLAVOURED WITH VANILLA AND TOPPED WITH A BRITTLE CARAMELIZED SUGAR CRUST.

SERVES SIX

INGREDIENTS

1 vanilla pod (bean)
1 litre/1¾ pints/4 cups double
  (heavy) cream
6 egg yolks
90g/3½oz/½ cup caster (superfine) sugar
30ml/2 tbsp almond or orange
  liqueur (optional)
75g/3oz/⅓ cup soft light brown sugar

1 Preheat the oven to 150°C/300°F/ Gas 2. Place six 125ml/4fl oz/½ cup ramekins in an ovenproof dish and set aside, then prepare the vanilla custard.

2 Split the vanilla pod and scrape the seeds into a pan. Add the cream and bring just to the boil, stirring frequently. Remove from the heat and cover. Set aside for 15–20 minutes.

3 In a bowl, whisk the egg yolks, caster sugar and liqueur, if using, until well blended. Whisk in the hot cream and strain into a large jug. Divide the custard equally among the ramekins.

4 Pour enough boiling water into the roasting tin to come about halfway up the sides of the ramekins. Cover the tin with foil and bake for about 30 minutes until the custards are just set. To test whether the custards are ready, push the point of a knife into the centre of one – if it comes out clean the custards are cooked. Remove the ramekins from the tin and leave to cool. Return to the dry roasting tin and chill.

5 Preheat the grill (broiler). Sprinkle the sugar evenly over the surface of each custard and grill (broil) for 30–60 seconds until the sugar melts and caramelizes, taking care not to let the sugar burn. Place in the fridge to chill and set the crust.

COOK'S TIP
It is best to make the custards the day before you wish to eat them.

CUSTARD TART WITH PLUMS

WHEN THIS TART IS MADE WITH REALLY RIPE, SWEET PLUMS, IT MAKES A WONDERFUL HOT OR COLD WEEKEND DESSERT. IT IS DELICIOUS SERVED WITH THICK CREAM OR ICE CREAM.

2 Flour a deep 18cm/7in square or 20cm/8in round loose-bottomed tin. Roll out the pastry and use to line the tin. This pastry is soft at this stage, so don't worry if you have to push it into shape. Chill for another 10–20 minutes.

3 Preheat the oven to 200°C/400°F/ Gas 6. Line the pastry case with greaseproof paper and fill with baking beans, then bake for 15 minutes. Remove the paper and beans, reduce the heat to 180°C/350°F/Gas 4 and bake for a further 5–10 minutes until the base is dry.

SERVES FOUR TO SIX

INGREDIENTS
175g/6oz/1½ cups plain (all-purpose) flour, sifted, plus pinch of salt
45ml/3 tbsp caster (superfine) sugar
115g/4oz/½ cup unsalted butter
2 eggs, plus 2 yolks
350g/12oz ripe plums
300ml/½ pint/1¼ cups milk
few drops of vanilla extract
thick cream or ice cream, to serve
flaked (sliced) almonds and icing (confectioner's) sugar, to decorate

1 Place the flour, salt, 15ml/1 tbsp of the sugar, the butter and one of the eggs in a food processor or blender and process until thoroughly combined. Turn out the mixture on to a clean, lightly floured surface and bring it together into a ball. Cover the pastry and leave for 10 minutes to rest.

VARIATIONS
This tart is equally delicious made with apricots, peaches or nectarines. Make a nutty pastry by replacing 15ml/1 tbsp of the flour with ground almonds.

4 Halve and stone the plums, and arrange them neatly in the pastry case. Whisk together the remaining egg and egg yolks with the sugar, the milk and vanilla extract and pour over the fruit.

5 Return the tart to the oven and bake for 25–30 minutes. When the custard is just firm to the touch, remove the tart from the oven and allow to cool. Sprinkle with toasted flaked almonds and dredge with icing sugar before serving. Add a generous dollop of cream or ice cream to each portion.

BAKED CARAMEL CUSTARD

MANY COUNTRIES HAVE THEIR OWN VERSION OF THIS CLASSIC DESSERT. KNOWN AS CRÈME CARAMEL IN FRANCE AND FLAN IN SPAIN, THIS CHILLED BAKED CUSTARD HAS A RICH CARAMEL FLAVOUR AND IS WONDERFUL WHEN FRESHLY MADE. SERVE IT WITH EXTRA THICK CREAM AND STRAWBERRIES.

SERVES SIX TO EIGHT

INGREDIENTS
  250g/9oz/1¼ cups sugar
  1 vanilla pod (bean)
  425ml/15fl oz/1¾ cups double
    (heavy) cream
  5 large eggs, plus 2 extra yolks
  thick cream and fresh strawberries,
    to serve

1 Put 175g/6oz/generous ¾ cup of the sugar in a small heavy-based saucepan with just enough water to moisten the sugar. Bring to the boil over a high heat, swirling the pan until the sugar is dissolved completely. Boil for about 5 minutes, without stirring, until the syrup turns a dark caramel colour.

2 Working quickly, pour the caramel into a 1 litre/1¾ pint/4 cup soufflé dish. Holding the dish with oven gloves, carefully swirl to coat the base and sides with the hot caramel mixture and set aside to cool.

3 Preheat the oven to 160°C/325°F/Gas 3. With a small sharp knife, carefully split the vanilla pod lengthways and scrape the black seeds into a saucepan. Add the cream and bring just to the boil over a medium-high heat, stirring frequently. Remove the pan from the heat, cover and set aside for about 20 minutes to cool.

4 In a bowl, whisk the eggs and egg yolks with the remaining sugar for 2–3 minutes until smooth and creamy.

5 Whisk in the hot cream and carefully strain the mixture into the caramel-lined dish. Cover tightly with foil.

VARIATION
For a special occasion, make individual baked custards in ramekin dishes. Coat 6–8 ramekins with the caramel and divide the custard mixture among them. Bake, in a roasting tin of water, for 25–30 minutes or until set. Slice the strawberries and marinate them in a little sugar and a liqueur or dessert wine, such as Amaretto or Muscat wine.

6 Place the dish in a roasting tin and pour in just enough boiling water to come halfway up the side of the dish.

7 Bake the custard for 40–45 minutes until just set. To test whether the custard is set, insert a knife about 5cm/2in from the edge; if it comes out clean, the custard should be ready.

8 Remove the soufflé dish from the roasting tin and leave to cool for at least 30 minutes, then place in the fridge and chill overnight.

9 To turn out, carefully run a sharp knife around the edge of the dish to loosen the custard.

10 Cover the dish with a serving plate and, holding them together very tightly, invert the dish and plate, allowing the custard to drop down on to the plate.

11 Gently lift one edge of the dish, allowing the caramel to run down over the sides and on to the plate, then carefully lift off the dish. Serve with thick cream and fresh strawberries.

COLD LEMON SOUFFLÉ WITH ALMONDS

TERRIFIC TO LOOK AT YET EASY TO MAKE, THIS REFRESHING DESSERT SOUFFLÉ IS LIGHT AND MOUTH-WATERING, IDEAL FOR THE END OF ANY MEAL.

SERVES SIX

INGREDIENTS
oil, for greasing
grated rind and juice of 3 large lemons
5 large eggs, separated
115g/4oz/½ cup caster
 (superfine) sugar
25ml/1½ tbsp powdered gelatine
450ml/¾ pint/scant 2 cups
 double (heavy) cream
For the almond topping
75g/3oz/¾ cup flaked (sliced) almonds
75g/3oz/¾ cup icing
 (confectioners') sugar

1 To make the soufflé collar, cut a strip of non-stick baking parchment long enough to fit around a 900ml/1½ pint/3¾ cup soufflé dish and wide enough to extend 7.5cm/3in above the rim. Fit the strip around the dish, tape, then tie it around the top of the dish with string.

2 Using a pastry brush, lightly coat the inside of the paper collar with oil.

3 Put the lemon rind and egg yolks in a bowl. Add 75g/3oz/6 tbsp of the caster sugar and whisk thoroughly until the mixture becomes light and creamy.

VARIATIONS
This soufflé is wonderfully refreshing when served semi-frozen. Place the undecorated, set soufflé in the freezer for about an hour. Just before serving, remove from the freezer and decorate with the caramelized almonds. You can also vary the flavour slightly by using the juice and rind of 5 limes.

4 Place the lemon juice in a small heatproof bowl and sprinkle over the gelatine. Set aside for 5 minutes, then place the bowl in a pan of simmering water. Heat, stirring occasionally, until the gelatine has dissolved. Cool slightly, then stir the gelatine and lemon juice into the egg yolk mixture.

5 In a separate bowl, lightly whip the cream to soft peaks. Fold into the egg yolk mixture and set aside.

6 Whisk the whites to stiff peaks. Gradually whisk in the remaining caster sugar until stiff and glossy. Quickly and lightly fold the whites into the yolk mixture. Pour into the prepared dish, smooth the surface and chill for 4–5 hours.

7 To make the almond topping, brush a baking sheet with oil. Preheat the grill (broiler). Scatter the almonds over the baking sheet and sift the icing sugar over. Grill (broil) until the nuts turn a rich golden colour and the sugar has caramelized.

8 Allow to cool, then remove the almond mixture from the tray with a palette knife and break it into pieces.

9 When the soufflé has set, carefully peel off the paper. If the paper does not come away easily, hold the blade of a knife against the set soufflé to help it keep its shape, if necessary. Scatter the caramelized almonds on top of the soufflé, to serve.

COOK'S TIP
To dissolve the gelatine more quickly, heat the lemon juice and gelatine in a microwave, on full power, in 30 second bursts, stirring between each burst, until it is fully dissolved.

BANANA WITH APRICOT CARAMEL TRIFLE

EVERYONE LOVES TRIFLE BUT IT DOESN'T NEED TO BE ALCOHOLIC TO BE DELICIOUS. GINGER CAKE
MAKES A DELICIOUS BASE, BUT YOU COULD USE YOUR FAMILY'S FAVOURITE FLAVOUR, IF YOU PREFER.
TOP WITH PLENTY OF WHIPPED CREAM.

SERVES SIX TO EIGHT

INGREDIENTS
    300ml/½ pint/1¼ cups milk
    1 vanilla pod (bean), or 4–5 drops
        vanilla extract
    45ml/3 tbsp caster (superfine) sugar
    20ml/4 tsp cornflour (cornstarch)
    3 egg yolks
    ¼ packet apricot or tangerine jelly
    60ml/4 tbsp apricot conserve
    175–225g/6–8oz ginger
        cake, cubed
    3 bananas, sliced, with one
        reserved for topping
    115g/4oz/½ cup sugar
    300ml/½ pint/1¼ cups double
        (heavy) cream
    a few drops of lemon juice

1 Add the milk to a small pan. Split the vanilla pod (if using) and scrape the seeds into the pan.

2 Add the vanilla pod, or vanilla extract, to the milk and bring just to the boil, then remove the pan from the heat. When the milk has cooled slightly, remove the vanilla pod (if using).

COOK'S TIP
Use whatever type of cake you prefer in the base of the trifle. Leftover Madeira cake, with its tangy citrus flavour, makes a perfect choice. Choose a jelly and conserve with flavours that complement those of your chosen cake: strawberry jelly and raspberry conserve are good with lemon cake, or try lemon jelly and peach conserve with a chocolate sponge.

3 Whisk together the sugar, cornflour and eggs until pale and creamy. Whisk in the milk and return the whole mixture to the pan. Heat to simmering point, stirring all the time, and cook gently over a low heat until the custard coats the back of a wooden spoon thickly.

4 Leave to cool, covered tightly with clear film. Ensure the clear film is pressed against the surface of the custard to prevent a skin forming.

5 Put the jelly, apricot conserve and 60ml/4 tbsp water in a small pan and heat gently until the jelly dissolves. Set aside until cool but not set.

VARIATION
For an adult-only version of this trifle, substitute a plainer sponge cake for the ginger cake. Before pouring the jelly mixture over the cubed cake, moisten the sponge with a little apricot brandy and a small glass of sweet dessert wine. If you choose to use a different flavoured jelly and conserve, try a different liqueur or brandy that will complement the flavour of the jelly and conserve.

6 Put the cubed cake in a deep serving bowl or dish and pour on the jelly mixture. Cover with sliced bananas, then the custard. Chill for 1–2 hours.

7 Melt the sugar in a small pan with 60ml/4 tbsp water and, when it has dissolved, cook until it is just turning golden. Immediately pour on to a sheet of foil and leave to harden, then break the caramel into pieces.

8 Whip the cream until it forms soft peaks and spread it over the custard. Chill for at least 2 hours, then top with the remaining sliced banana, dipped into lemon juice, and the cracked caramel pieces.

FLOATING ISLANDS

THE FRENCH NAME FOR THIS DISH IS OEUFS À LA NEIGE, MEANING SNOW EGGS. TRADITIONALLY THE MERINGUES ARE POACHED IN MILK, WHICH IS THEN USED TO MAKE THE RICH CUSTARD SAUCE. HOWEVER, THIS METHOD USES WATER FOR POACHING, WHICH GIVES A LIGHTER RESULT.

SERVES FOUR TO SIX

INGREDIENTS
   1 vanilla pod (bean)
   600ml/1 pint/2½ cups milk
   8 egg yolks
   50g/2oz/¼ cup granulated
      (white) sugar
For the meringues
   4 large egg whites
   1.5ml/¼ tsp cream of tartar
   225g/8oz/1¼ cups caster
      (superfine) sugar
For the caramel
   150g/5oz/¾ cup granulated sugar

1 Using a knife with a sharp point, split the vanilla pod lengthways and scrape the seeds into a pan. Add the milk and bring to the boil over a medium-high heat, stirring often. Remove the pan from the heat and cover. Set aside for 15–20 minutes to cool slightly.

2 Whisk the egg yolks and sugar for 2–3 minutes until thick and creamy. Remove the vanilla pod from the hot milk, then whisk the milk into the egg mixture and return to the pan.

3 With a wooden spoon, stir the sauce over a medium-low heat until it begins to thicken and coats the back of the spoon; do not allow the custard to boil or it may curdle.

4 Strain the custard into a chilled bowl, allow to cool, stirring occasionally, then chill until ready to serve.

5 Half-fill a large frying pan or wide pan with water and bring just to simmering point. In a clean grease-free bowl, whisk the egg whites slowly until they are frothy. Add the cream of tartar, increase the speed and continue whisking until they form soft peaks. Gradually sprinkle over the caster sugar, about 30ml/2 tbsp at a time, and whisk until the whites are stiff and glossy.

6 Using two tablespoons, form egg-shaped meringues and slide them into the water – you may need to work in batches. Poach them for 2–3 minutes, turning once, until the meringue is just firm. Use a slotted spoon to transfer the meringues from the pan to a baking sheet lined with kitchen paper to drain.

7 Pour the cold custard into shallow individual serving dishes or plates and arrange the meringues on top.

8 To make the caramel, put the sugar into a small heavy-based pan with 45ml/3 tbsp of water. Bring the dampened sugar to the boil over a high heat, carefully swirling the pan to dissolve it. Do not allow to boil until the sugar is completely dissolved, then boil, without stirring, until the syrup turns a dark caramel colour.

9 Working quickly before it hardens, drizzle the caramel over the poached meringues and custard in a zigzag pattern. Serve cold.

COOK'S TIP
Do not make the caramel too far ahead or it will soften as it sits on the moist meringues. If you do not have a vanilla pod, you can use 5ml/1 tsp vanilla extract instead.

APPLE AND ROSE PETAL SNOW

THIS IS A LOVELY, LIGHT AND REFRESHING DESSERT, WHICH IS IDEAL TO MAKE WHEN THE ORCHARDS ARE GROANING WITH APPLES. THE ROSE PETALS GIVE A DELICATE FRAGRANCE BUT OTHER EDIBLE PETALS SUCH AS HONEYSUCKLE, LAVENDER AND GERANIUM COULD ALSO BE USED.

SERVES FOUR

INGREDIENTS
  2 large cooking apples
  150ml/¼ pint/⅔ cup thick
    apple juice
  30ml/1 tbsp rose water
  2 egg whites
  75g/3oz/generous ⅓ cup caster
    (superfine) sugar, or to taste
  a few rose petals from an
    unsprayed rose
  crisp biscuits (cookies) or brandy
    snaps, to serve

COOK'S TIP
This recipe uses raw egg whites but it
can also be made with a cooked
meringue mixture instead.

1 Peel and chop the apples and cook
with the apple juice until soft. Sieve,
add the rose water and leave to cool.

2 Whisk the egg whites until peaking,
then gently whisk in the sugar. Gently
fold together the apple and egg whites.
Stir in most of the rose petals.

3 Spoon the snow into four glasses and
chill. Serve topped with the remaining
petals and crisp biscuits or brandy snaps.

VARIATION
To make sugared rose petals, brush each
petal with beaten egg white, scatter with
granulated sugar and leave to dry.

MANGO AND TANGERINE SORBET

MANGO MAKES THE EASIEST AND MOST DELICIOUS OF SORBETS. IT DOESN'T NEED A SUGAR SYRUP YET STILL GIVES A MELT-IN-THE-MOUTH CONSISTENCY. IF YOU CAN, USE THE SMALL, YELLOW INDIAN MANGOES; THEIR FLAVOUR IS EXQUISITE AND THEIR FLESH IS AMAZINGLY PERFUMED.

MAKES 450ML/¾ PINT/1¾ CUPS

INGREDIENTS
  4 tangerines
  1 lemon
  90g/3½oz/½ cup caster
    (superfine) sugar
  1 large ripe mango
  3 egg whites
  fresh raspberries, to serve

COOK'S TIP
Always treat hot syrups with great care as
they can cause bad burns if splashed on
to the skin.

VARIATION
For a more elegant dessert, serve scoops
of the sorbet in brandy snap baskets or
chocolate cases. Scatter with fresh
berries, to serve.

1 Squeeze the juice from the tangerines
and lemon into a small saucepan. Stir
in the sugar.

2 Gently heat the mixture and bring to
simmering point, skimming constantly.
Still stirring, simmer gently until the
mixture begins to turn slightly syrupy,
then remove the pan from the heat and
leave to cool slightly.

3 Purée the mango in a food processor
and stir in the syrup. Whisk the egg
whites until holding soft peaks and fold
into the mango purée. Freeze, whisking
every half hour for 3–4 hours, or churn
in an ice-cream machine.

4 Serve the sorbet immediately, or leave
it to freeze completely then allow
15–20 minutes at room temperature
before serving with raspberries.

RICH VANILLA ICE CREAM

This classic vanilla ice cream is quite superb. Serve it on its own or use as the base for other ices and desserts.

MAKES 750ML/1¼ PINTS/3 CUPS

INGREDIENTS

300ml/½ pint/1¼ cups single (light) cream
1 vanilla pod (bean)
3 egg yolks
45ml/3 tbsp caster (superfine) sugar
10ml/2 tsp cornflour (cornstarch)
300ml/½ pint/1¼ cups double (heavy) cream, whipped

VARIATION

For chocolate ice cream, add 175g/6oz plain (semisweet) chocolate, melted, and 30ml/2 tbsp cocoa powder to the custard.

1 Put the cream in a small pan. Split the vanilla pod and scrape out the tiny seeds. Add them to the cream with the pod. Bring the cream just to the boil, then turn off the heat.

2 Whisk together the eggs, sugar and cornflour until pale and creamy. Remove the vanilla pod from the cream and whisk into the egg mixture. Return the mixture to the pan and bring to a simmer, stirring all the time. Cook gently until the custard coats the back of a wooden spoon.

3 Leave the custard to cool completely, then whisk well and fold in the whipped cream. Spoon it into a freezer container and freeze, whisking once every hour for 2–3 hours, or churn in an ice-cream maker until almost frozen, then transfer to the freezer.

ICED RASPBERRY PAVLOVA ROULADE

THIS MELT-IN-THE-MOUTH MERINGUE, ROLLED AROUND VANILLA CREAM AND LUSCIOUS RASPBERRIES, IS A STAR DINNER-PARTY ATTRACTION, AND IS SURPRISINGLY QUICK AND SIMPLE TO MAKE.

SERVES SIX TO EIGHT

INGREDIENTS
10ml/2 tsp cornflour (cornstarch)
225g/8oz/generous 1 cup caster
  (superfine) sugar
4 egg whites, at room temperature
icing (confectioners') sugar, sifted
300ml/½ pint/1¼ cups double
  (heavy) cream or whipping cream
a few drops of vanilla extract
175g/6oz/1 cup raspberries, partly
  frozen, plus extra to serve

1 Line a 33 × 23cm/13 × 9in Swiss roll tin with non-stick baking paper. Sift the cornflour into a bowl and blend evenly with the sugar.

2 Using a balloon whisk or hand-held electric beaters, whisk the egg whites in a clean mixing bowl until they form stiff peaks, but are not dry and crumbly.

3 Gradually whisk in the caster sugar, a few spoonfuls at a time, until the mixture becomes stiff and glossy.

4 Spoon the mixture into the prepared tin and flatten the top. Place in a cold oven and turn it to 150°C/300°F/Gas 2. Cook for 1 hour until the top is crisp and the meringue still feels springy (if it appears to be colouring too early while cooking, reduce the temperature).

5 Turn out on to a double sheet of greaseproof paper sprinkled with sifted icing sugar and leave to cool.

6 Meanwhile, whip the cream with the vanilla extract and stir in the partly frozen raspberries. Freeze the mixture until required.

7 When the meringue has cooled, carefully spread the cream over it, then roll up, using the paper as a support. Freeze for about 1 hour before serving, sprinkled with more icing sugar and extra raspberries.

COOK'S TIP
The filling can be as varied as you wish. Try flavouring the cream with liqueur or home-made lemon curd, or fill with softened ice cream, then return the roulade to the freezer immediately.

CHOCOLATE CHESTNUT ROULADE

This combination of intense flavours produces a very rich dessert, so serve it well chilled and in thin slices. It slices better when it is very cold.

SERVES TEN TO TWELVE

INGREDIENTS

oil, for greasing
175g/6oz dark (unsweetened)
  chocolate, chopped
30ml/2 tbsp unsweetened
  cocoa powder, sifted, plus extra
50ml/2fl oz/¼ cup freshly brewed
  strong coffee or espresso
6 eggs, separated
75g/3oz/6 tbsp caster
  (superfine) sugar
pinch of cream of tartar
5ml/1 tsp vanilla extract
glacé chestnuts, to decorate
For the chestnut cream filling
475ml/16fl oz/2 cups double
  (heavy) cream
30ml/2 tbsp rum
350g/12oz can sweetened
  chestnut purée
115g/4oz dark chocolate, grated
thick cream, to serve

1 Preheat the oven to 180°C/350°F/
Gas 4. Grease the base and sides of a
39 × 27 × 2.5cm/15½ × 10½ × 1in
Swiss roll tin. Line with non-stick baking
paper, allowing a 2.5cm/1in overhang.

2 Melt the chocolate in the top of a
double boiler, over a low heat, stirring
often. Set aside. Dissolve the cocoa in
the coffee. Stir to make a smooth paste.
Set aside.

COOK'S TIP
Beating egg whites should be the last
step in making cake mixtures. Once
beaten, they should be folded in at once.

3 In an electric mixer or in a bowl using
a whisk, beat the egg yolks with half the
sugar for about 3–5 minutes until pale
and thick. Slowly beat in the melted
chocolate and cocoa-coffee paste until
just blended.

4 In another bowl, beat the egg whites
and cream of tartar until stiff peaks
form. Sprinkle the remaining sugar over
in two batches and beat until stiff and
glossy, then beat in the vanilla extract.

5 Stir a spoonful of the whisked whites
into the chocolate mixture to lighten it,
then fold in the remainder.

6 Spoon the mixture into the tin and
level the top. Bake for 20–25 minutes
or until the cake springs back when
lightly pressed with the fingertips.

7 Meanwhile, dust a clean dish towel
with the extra cocoa powder. As soon as
the cake is cooked, carefully turn it out
on to the towel and gently peel off the
greaseproof paper from the base.
Starting at a narrow end, roll the cake
and towel together Swiss-roll fashion.
Cool completely.

8 To make the filling, whip the cream
and rum or liqueur until soft peaks
form. Beat a spoonful of cream into the
chestnut purée to lighten it, then fold in
the remaining cream and most of the
grated chocolate. Reserve a quarter of
the chestnut cream mixture.

9 To assemble the roulade, unroll the
cake and spread with the filling, to
within 2.5cm/1in of the edges. Gently
roll it up, using the towel for support.

10 Place the roulade, seam-side down,
on a serving plate. Spoon the reserved
chestnut cream into a small icing bag
and pipe rosettes along the top. Dust
with more cocoa and decorate with
glacé chestnuts and grated chocolate.

HOT PUDDINGS

There is nothing better than a hot pudding at the end of a meal. The classic French batter pudding, Black Cherry Clafoutis, or a wonderful steamed Chocolate Pudding with Rum Custard are great on a cold winter evening. Warm and fluffy Zabaglione and Summer Berries in Warm Sabayon Glaze offer a lighter, yet equally tempting, alternative. Children love hot desserts, too, and this chapter includes a whole range of puddings that are sure to be popular with the whole family. Apricot Panettone Pudding provides a twist on the traditional bread and butter pudding, and Rhubarb Meringue Pie combines the sharp, tangy flavour of rhubarb with mouth-watering meringue and crisp pastry.

PRUNE TART WITH CUSTARD FILLING

PRUNES AND ARMAGNAC MAKE A FANTASTIC COMBINATION BUT, IF YOU PREFER, REPLACE THE LIQUEUR WITH FRESH ORANGE JUICE.

3 Turn out on a clean, lightly floured surface and bring the mixture together into a ball. Leave for 10 minutes to rest.

4 Flour a 28 x 18cm/11 x 7in loose-based tin. Roll out the pastry and line the tin; don't worry if you have to push it into shape, as this pastry is soft and easy to mould. Chill for 10–20 minutes.

5 Line the pastry case with greaseproof paper and fill with baking beans, then bake for 15 minutes. Remove the paper and beans, and bake for 10–15 minutes. Brush the base of the pastry with the reserved egg white while it is still hot. Set aside to cool slightly.

6 Bring the milk and vanilla extract to the boil. In a bowl, whisk the egg yolks and 40g/1½oz/3 tbsp sugar until thick, pale and fluffy, then whisk in the cornflour. Strain in the milk and whisk until there are no lumps.

SERVES SIX TO EIGHT

INGREDIENTS
225g/8oz/1 cup pitted prunes
50ml/2fl oz/¼ cup brandy
175g/6oz/1½ cups plain (all-purpose) flour, sifted, plus extra for dusting
pinch of salt
90g/3½oz/scant ½ cup caster (superfine) sugar
115g/4oz/½ cup unsalted butter, at room temperature
1 egg, plus 4 egg yolks
300ml/½ pint/1¼ cups milk
a few drops of vanilla extract
15g/½oz/2 tbsp cornflour (cornstarch)
25g/1oz/¼ cup flaked (sliced) almonds
icing (confectioners') sugar, sifted
thick cream, to serve

1 Place the prunes in a bowl with the brandy and leave in a warm place to soak.

2 Preheat the oven to 200°C/400°F/ Gas 6. Place the flour, salt, 50g/2oz/ ¼ cup sugar, butter and egg, reserving 5ml/1 tsp egg white, in a food processor and process until blended.

7 Return to the pan and bring to the boil, whisking all the time to remove any lumps. Cook for about 2 minutes until thick and smooth, then set aside to cool. Press clear film on to the surface of the custard to prevent a skin forming.

8 Stir any prune liquid into the custard, then spread over the pastry case. Arrange the prunes on top, sprinkle with the flaked almonds and icing sugar, and return to the oven for 10 minutes until golden and glazed. Remove from the oven and leave to cool. Serve hot or at room temperature with cream.

BLACK CHERRY CLAFOUTIS

*CLAFOUTIS IS A BATTER PUDDING THAT ORIGINATED IN THE LIMOUSIN AREA OF CENTRAL FRANCE.
IT IS OFTEN MADE WITH CREAM AND TRADITIONALLY USES SLIGHTLY TART BLACK CHERRIES, ALTHOUGH
OTHER SOFT FRUITS CAN ALSO GIVE DELICIOUS RESULTS.*

SERVES SIX

INGREDIENTS
    butter, for greasing
    450g/1lb/2 cups black cherries, pitted
    25g/1oz/¼ cup plain
        (all-purpose) flour
    50g/2oz/½ cup icing (confectioners')
        sugar, plus extra for dusting
    4 eggs, beaten
    250ml/8fl oz/1 cup full-fat
        (whole) milk
    30ml/2 tbsp cherry liqueur, such as
        kirsch or maraschino

1 Preheat the oven to 180°C/350°F/
Gas 4. Generously grease a 1.2 litre/
2 pint/5 cup dish and add the cherries.

2 Sift the flour and icing sugar into a
large mixing bowl, then gradually whisk
in the beaten eggs until the mixture is
smooth. Whisk in the milk until well
blended, then stir in the liqueur.

3 Pour the batter into the baking dish.
Transfer to the oven and bake for about
40 minutes, or until just set and light
golden brown. Insert a knife into the
centre of the pudding to test if it is
cooked in the middle; the blade should
come out clean.

4 Allow the pudding to cool for at least
15 minutes. Dust liberally with icing
sugar just before serving, either warm
or at room temperature.

VARIATIONS
Try other liqueurs in this dessert.
Almond-flavoured liqueur is delicious
teamed with cherries, while hazelnut,
raspberry or orange liqueurs will also
work well. Other fruits that can be used
in this pudding include blackberries,
blueberries, plums and apricots.

RHUBARB MERINGUE PIE

*THE SHARP TANG OF RHUBARB WITH ITS SWEET MERINGUE TOPPING WILL REALLY TANTALIZE THE
TASTE BUDS. THIS PUDDING IS DELICIOUS HOT OR COLD WITH CREAM OR VANILLA ICE CREAM.*

3 Meanwhile, put the rhubarb, 75g/3oz/ 6 tbsp of the remaining sugar and the orange rind in a pan. Cover with a lid and cook over a low heat until the rhubarb is tender.

4 Remove the beans and paper from the pastry case, then brush all over with a little of the remaining egg yolk. Bake for 10–15 minutes, until the pastry is crisp.

5 Blend together the cornflour and the orange juice in a small bowl. Off the heat, stir the cornflour mixture into the cooked rhubarb, then bring to the boil, stirring constantly until thickened. Cook for a further 1–2 minutes. Cool slightly, then beat in the remaining egg yolks. Pour into the flan case.

6 Whisk the egg whites until they form soft peaks, then whisk in the remaining sugar, 15ml/1 tbsp at a time, whisking well after each addition.

7 Swirl the meringue over the filling to cover completely. Bake for 25 minutes until golden. Serve warm, or leave to cool for about 30 minutes and serve, with whipped cream.

SERVES SIX

INGREDIENTS
 200g/7oz/1¾ cups plain (all-purpose)
   flour, plus extra for flouring
 25g/1oz/⅓ cup ground walnuts
 115g/4oz/½ cup butter, diced
 275g/10oz/generous 1½ cups
   caster (superfine) sugar
 4 egg yolks
 675g/1½ lb rhubarb, cut into
   small pieces
 finely grated rind and juice of
   3 blood or navel oranges
 75ml/5 tbsp cornflour (cornstarch)
 3 egg whites
 whipped cream, to serve

1 Sift the flour into a bowl and add the ground walnuts. Rub in the butter until the mixture resembles very fine bread-crumbs. Stir in 30ml/2 tbsp of the sugar with 1 egg yolk beaten with 15ml/1 tbsp water. Mix to a firm dough. Turn out on to a floured surface and knead lightly. Wrap in a polythene bag and chill for at least 30 minutes.

2 Preheat the oven to 190°C/375°F/ Gas 5. Roll out the pastry on a lightly floured surface and use to line a 23cm/ 9in fluted flan tin. Prick the base with a fork. Line the pastry with greaseproof paper and fill with baking beans, then bake for 15 minutes.

PINEAPPLE BAKED ALASKA

MOST CHILDREN LOVE THE SURPRISE OF THIS CLASSIC PUDDING — HOT MERINGUE WITH ICE-COLD ICE CREAM INSIDE. HERE'S A NEW VARIATION TO TRY OUT ON THEM.

SERVES THREE TO FOUR

INGREDIENTS
    3 large egg whites
    150g/5oz/¾ cup caster (superfine)
      sugar
    25g/1oz desiccated (dry unsweetened
      shredded) coconut
    175–225g/6–8oz piece of ready-made
      cake, such as ginger or chocolate
    6 slices ripe, peeled pineapple
    500ml/17fl oz/2¼ cups vanilla ice
      cream, in a brick
    a few cherries or figs, to decorate

1 Preheat the oven to 230°C/450°F/
Gas 8. Whisk the egg whites until stiff,
then whisk in the sugar until the
mixture is stiff. Fold in the coconut.

2 Slice the cake into two thick layers
the same rectangular shape as the ice
cream. Cut the pineapple into triangles
or quarters, cutting it over the cake to
catch any drips. On a baking tray,
arrange the fruit on top of one slice of
cake. Top with the ice cream and then
the second layer of cake.

3 Spread the meringue over the cake
and ice cream, and bake in the oven for
5–7 minutes, or until turning golden.
Serve immediately, topped with fruit.

COOK'S TIP
Do not use soft-scoop ice cream for this
dessert as it will soften too quickly.

HOT CHOCOLATE SOUFFLÉS

THESE RICH, INDIVIDUAL SOUFFLÉS HAVE THE MEREST HINT OF ORANGE IN THEM, AND ARE DIVINE WITH THE WHITE CHOCOLATE SAUCE POURED INTO THE MIDDLE.

SERVES SIX

INGREDIENTS
  45ml/3 tbsp caster (superfine) sugar,
    plus extra for dusting
  175g/6oz plain (semisweet)
    chocolate, chopped
  150g/5oz/⅔ cup unsalted butter, cut in
    small pieces, plus extra for greasing
  4 large eggs, separated
  30ml/2 tbsp orange liqueur (optional)
  1.5ml/¼ tsp cream of tartar
  icing (confectioners') sugar, for dusting
For the white chocolate sauce
  75g/3oz white chocolate, chopped
  90ml/6 tbsp whipping cream
  15–30ml/1–2 tbsp orange liqueur
  grated rind of ½ orange

3 Preheat the oven to 220ºC/425ºF/ Gas 7. In a large, grease-free bowl, whisk the egg whites slowly until frothy. Add the cream of tartar, increase the speed and whisk until the whites form soft peaks. Gradually sprinkle over the caster sugar, 15ml/1 tbsp at a time, whisking until the whites become stiff and glossy.

4 Stir a third of the whites into the cooled chocolate mixture to lighten it, then pour the mixture over the remaining whites.

6 To make the white chocolate sauce, put the chopped white chocolate and the cream into a small saucepan. Place over a very low heat and warm, stirring constantly until melted and smooth. Remove from the heat and stir in the liqueur and orange rind, then pour into a serving jug and keep warm.

1 Generously grease six 150ml/¼ pint/ ⅔ cup ramekins. Sprinkle each with a little caster sugar and tap out any excess. Place the ramekins on a baking sheet.

2 Melt the chocolate and butter in a bowl placed over a pan of simmering water, stirring constantly. Remove from the heat and cool slightly, then beat in the egg yolks and orange liqueur, if using. Set aside, stirring occasionally.

5 Using a rubber spatula or large metal spoon, gently fold the sauce into the whites, cutting down to the bottom, then along the sides and up to the top in a semicircular motion until the chocolate mixture and egg whites are just combined; don't worry about a few white streaks. Spoon the combined mixture into the prepared dishes.

VARIATION
Like orange, coffee complements the flavour of chocolate perfectly. Try using a coffee liqueur, such as Kahlúa or Tia Maria, instead of the orange liqueur in the soufflé mixture and sauce.

7 Bake the soufflés in the preheated oven for 10–12 minutes until risen and set, but still slightly wobbly in the centre. Dust with icing sugar and serve immediately with the warm white chocolate sauce.

COOK'S TIP
These soufflés are ideal for serving at a dinner party because they can be prepared in advance, ready for baking at the last minute. Follow steps 1–5 above, then tightly cover the uncooked soufflés with clear film. Set aside in a cool, but not cold, place until ready to cook. If the soufflés become too cold while waiting to be cooked, allow an extra 2–3 minutes cooking time.

CHOCOLATE PUDDING <u>WITH</u> RUM CUSTARD

WITH MELTING MOMENTS OF CHOCOLATE IN EVERY MOUTHFUL, THESE LITTLE PUDDINGS WON'T LAST LONG. THE RUM CUSTARD TURNS THEM INTO A MORE ADULT PUDDING; FOR A FAMILY DESSERT, FLAVOUR THE CUSTARD WITH VANILLA OR ORANGE RIND INSTEAD.

SERVES SIX

INGREDIENTS
    115g/4oz/½ cup butter, plus extra
      for greasing
    115g/4oz/½ cup soft light
      brown sugar
    2 eggs, beaten
    a few drops of vanilla extract
    45ml/3 tbsp unsweetened cocoa
      powder, sifted
    115g/4oz/1 cup self-raising
      (self-rising) flour
    75g/3oz cooking chocolate
      (unsweetened), chopped
    a little melting milk, warmed
For the rum custard
    250ml/8fl oz/1 cup milk
    15ml/1 tbsp caster (superfine) sugar
    2 egg yolks
    10ml/2 tsp cornflour (cornstarch)
    30–45ml/2–3 tbsp rum

1 Lightly grease a 1.2 litre/2 pint/5 cup pudding basin or six individual dariole moulds. Cream the butter and sugar until pale and creamy. Gently blend in the eggs and the vanilla extract.

2 Sift together the cocoa and flour, and fold gently into the egg mixture with the chopped chocolate and sufficient milk to give a soft dropping consistency.

3 Spoon the mixture into the basin or moulds, cover with buttered greaseproof paper and tie down. Fill a pan with 2.5–5cm/1–2in water, place the puddings in the pan, cover with a lid and bring to the boil. Steam the large pudding for 1½–2 hours and the individual puddings for 45–50 minutes, topping up with water if necessary. When firm, turn out on to warm plates.

4 To make the rum custard, bring the milk and sugar to the boil. Whisk together the egg yolks and cornflour, then pour on the hot milk, whisking constantly. Return the mixture to the pan and stir continuously while it slowly comes back to the boil. Allow the sauce to simmer gently as it thickens, stirring all the time. Remove from the heat and stir in the rum.

APRICOT PANETTONE PUDDING

THE COMBINATION OF THE LIGHT ITALIAN FRUIT BREAD, APRICOTS AND PECAN NUTS PRODUCES A WONDERFULLY RICH VERSION OF TRADITIONAL BREAD-AND-BUTTER PUDDING.

2 Pour the milk into a small saucepan and add the vanilla extract. Warm the milk over a medium heat until it just simmers. In a large bowl, mix together the beaten egg and maple syrup, grate in the nutmeg, then whisk in the hot milk.

3 Preheat the oven to 200°C/400°F/ Gas 6. Pour the milk mixture over the panettone, lightly pressing down each slice so that it is totally submerged in the mixture. Set the dish aside and leave the pudding to stand for at least 10 minutes.

4 Scatter the reserved pecan nuts over the top and sprinkle with the demerara sugar and nutmeg. Bake for about 40 minutes until risen and golden.

COOK'S TIP
Panettone is a sweet Italian yeast bread made with raisins, citron, pine nuts and star anise. It is traditionally served at Christmas and is easier to obtain at that time of year. If it is not available, use any sweet yeasted fruit loaf instead.

SERVES SIX

INGREDIENTS
 unsalted butter, for greasing
 350g/12oz panettone, sliced
  into triangles
 25g/1oz/¼ cup pecan nuts
 75g/3oz/⅓ cup ready-to-eat dried
  apricots, chopped
 500ml/17fl oz/2¼ cups semi-
  skimmed (low-fat) milk
 5ml/1 tsp vanilla extract
 1 large egg, beaten
 30ml/2 tbsp maple syrup
 2.5ml/½ tsp grated nutmeg, plus
  extra for sprinkling
 demerara (raw) sugar, for sprinkling

1 Grease a 1 litre/1¾ pint/4 cup baking dish. Arrange half the panettone in the base of the dish, scatter over half the pecan nuts and all the dried apricots, then add another layer of panettone on top, spreading it as evenly as you can.

CAKES AND BAKES

Eggs are an essential ingredient in cakes and bakes, and can help to create light and fluffy sponges, moist fruit cakes, crisp biscuits and rich breads. Eggs help the classic whisked sponge used in Fresh Fruit Genoese Sponge, Almond and Raspberry Swiss Roll and Angel Food Cake to rise beautifully, giving them an incredibly light texture. Frosted Carrot and Parsnip Cake uses not only eggs in the deliciously moist crumb, but also lightly cooked whisked egg whites for the mouth-watering meringue topping. Whole eggs are used to enrich breads, such as Honey and Saffron Bread, and Hungarian Fruit Bread, while eggs with dyed bright red shells are used to decorate the traditional Greek Easter Egg Bread.

FRESH FRUIT GENOESE SPONGE

GENOESE IS THE ORIGINAL FATLESS SPONGE, WHICH CAN BE USED FOR LUXURY GÂTEAUX AND SWISS ROLLS. IT SHOULD BE EATEN QUICKLY, AS IT DOES NOT STORE WELL.

SERVES EIGHT TO TEN

INGREDIENTS
oil or butter, for greasing
175g/6oz/1½ cups plain (all-purpose)
  flour, sifted
pinch of salt
4 eggs
115g/4oz/½ cup caster
  (superfine) sugar
90ml/6 tbsp orange-flavoured liqueur,
  such as Cointreau or Curaçao
For the filling and topping
600ml/1 pint/2½ cups double
  (heavy) cream
60ml/4 tbsp vanilla sugar
450g/1lb/4 cups fresh soft fruit, such
  as raspberries, strawberries,
  blueberries, cherries and redcurrants
150g/5oz/1¼ cups shelled pistachio
  nuts, finely chopped
60ml/4 tbsp apricot jam, warmed
  and sieved (strained)

1 Preheat the oven to 180°C/350°F/Gas 4. Grease a 21cm/8½in round springform cake tin (pan), line the base with baking parchment and grease the paper.

2 Sift the flour and salt together three times, then set aside.

3 Place the eggs and sugar in a mixing bowl and beat with an electric mixer for about 10 minutes or until thick and pale.

COOK'S TIP
If you wish to make the Genoese sponge a few days before you need it, it can be frozen. Allow to thaw at room temperature for several hours before filling.

4 Sift the pre-sifted flour and salt into the mixing bowl with the egg and sugar mixture, then fold together very gently. Carefully transfer the cake mixture to the prepared tin.

5 Bake in the centre of the oven for 30–35 minutes or until a skewer inserted into the centre of the cake comes out clean.

6 Leave the cake in the tin for about 5 minutes, then turn out on to a wire rack, peel off the lining paper and leave to cool completely.

7 Carefully cut the cake in half horizontally to create two layers. Place the bottom layer on a serving plate; then sprinkle the orange-flavoured liqueur over the cut side of each cake.

VARIATION
Because a Genoese sponge is made with no added fat, it makes a good choice for those who are following a low-fat diet. Replace the whipped cream filling with low-fat Greek (US strained plain) yogurt and pile on the fresh fruit.

8 Place the double cream and vanilla sugar in a large mixing bowl and beat together with an electric mixer until the mixture stands up in peaks.

9 Spread two-thirds of the cream mixture over the bottom layer of the cake and top with half of the soft fruit.

10 Carefully place the second half of the cake on top of the layer of cream and fruit and spread the remaining cream over the top.

11 Arrange the remaining fresh fruit on top of the cake and sprinkle with the chopped pistachio nuts. If liked, lightly glaze the top layer of fruit with the warmed apricot jam, then serve.

ALMOND AND RASPBERRY SWISS ROLL

*THIS LIGHT AND AIRY WHISKED SPONGE CAKE IS ROLLED UP WITH A RICH AND MOUTH-WATERING
FRESH CREAM AND RASPBERRY FILLING, MAKING A DELICIOUS TEA-TIME TREAT.*

SERVES EIGHT

INGREDIENTS
    oil, for greasing
    1 quantity Genoese sponge mixture,
      replacing 25g/1oz/2 tbsp plain
      (all-purpose) flour with 25g/1oz/
      2 tbsp ground almonds
    a little caster (superfine) sugar
    225ml/8fl oz/1 cup double
      (heavy) cream
    275g/10oz/1½ cups fresh raspberries
    16 flaked (sliced) almonds, toasted,
      to decorate

1 Preheat the oven to 200°C/400°F/
Gas 6. Grease and line a 33 × 23cm/
13 × 9in Swiss roll tin (jelly roll pan).

2 Spoon the Genoese sponge mixture
into the prepared Swiss roll tin and
bake for 10–12 minutes, until well risen
and springy to the touch.

3 Lay a sheet of baking parchment on a
flat surface and sprinkle liberally with
caster sugar. Turn out the cake on to
the greaseproof paper, and leave to cool
with the tin still in place.

4 Lift the tin off the cooled cake and
carefully peel away the lining paper
from the base of the cake.

5 Reserve a little of the cream for
decoration, if you like, then whip the
rest until it holds its shape. Fold in
250g/9oz/1¼ cups of the raspberries,
and spread the cream and raspberry
mixture over the cooled cake, leaving a
narrow border.

6 Carefully roll up the cake from a
narrow end to form a Swiss roll, using
the greaseproof paper to lift the sponge.
Sprinkle liberally with caster sugar.

7 Decorate the Swiss roll, if you like.
Whip the reserved cream until it just
holds its shape, and spoon it along the
top of the cake. Place the reserved
raspberries and toasted flaked almonds
on top of the cream and serve, or,
simply slice the Swiss roll and serve
with the raspberries and almonds.

COOK'S TIP
Do not leave the sponge to cool for too
long as it will be difficult to roll. If you
do not want to fill it immediately, cover it
with baking parchment, roll up loosely,
and leave until ready to fill.

MADEIRA CAKE WITH LEMON SYRUP

THIS SUGAR-CRUSTED CAKE IS SOAKED IN LEMON SYRUP, SO IT STAYS MOIST AND IS INFUSED WITH TANGY CITRUS FLAVOUR. SERVE IT SLICED WITH TEA.

SERVES TEN

INGREDIENTS

250g/9oz/1 cup plus 2 tbsp
    butter, softened
225g/8oz/generous 1 cup
    caster (superfine) sugar
5 eggs
275g/10oz/2½ cups plain
    (all-purpose) flour, sifted
10ml/2 tsp baking powder
salt
For the sugar crust
    60ml/4 tbsp lemon juice
    15ml/1 tbsp golden (light corn) syrup
    30ml/2 tbsp granulated (white) sugar

COOK'S TIP
Make double the quantity of cake.
Omit the syrup from one and leave plain.
Simply cool, wrap and freeze.

1 Preheat the oven to 180°C/350°F/ Gas 4. Grease a 1kg/2¼lb loaf tin (pan). Beat the butter and sugar until light and creamy, then gradually beat in the eggs.

2 Mix the sifted flour, baking powder and salt, and fold in gently. Spoon into the prepared tin, level the top and bake for 1¼ hours, until a skewer pushed into the middle comes out clean.

3 Remove the cake from the oven and, while still warm and in the tin, use a skewer to pierce it several times right the way through. Warm together the lemon juice and syrup, add the sugar and immediately spoon over the cake, so the flavoured syrup soaks through but leaves some sugar crystals on the top. Chill the cake for several hours or overnight before serving.

ANGEL FOOD CAKE

THIS IS AN AMERICAN CLASSIC. IT IS SIMILAR TO A WHISKED SPONGE CAKE; THE TEXTURE IS SPRINGY, BUT SLIGHTLY STICKY, AND THE COLOUR IS SNOWY WHITE. THE CREAM OF TARTAR HELPS TO STIFFEN THE EGG WHITES, AND THE ADDITION OF THE SUGAR FORMS A LIGHT MERINGUE MIXTURE.

SERVES TWENTY

INGREDIENTS
   65g/2½oz/5 tbsp plain (all-piurpose)
     flour, sifted
   15ml/1 tbsp cornflour (cornstarch)
   225g/8oz/generous 1 cup caster
     (superfine) sugar
   10 egg whites
   5ml/1 tsp cream of tartar
   7.5ml/1½ tsp vanilla extract
For the frosting
   115g/4oz/½ cup caster
     (superfine) sugar
   2 egg whites
   10ml/2 tsp golden (light corn) syrup
   2.5ml/½ tsp vanilla extract
   grated rind of one orange, to decorate

2 In a large, grease-free bowl, whisk the egg whites with the cream of tartar until stiff. Gradually whisk in the remaining sugar, 15ml/1 tbsp at a time, until the mixture becomes thick and glossy.

5 Slowly pour the syrup, in a steady stream, into the centre of the egg whites, whisking continuously, until the mixture becomes thick and glossy. Beat in the golden syrup and vanilla extract, and continue beating for 5 minutes until the frosting is cooled.

1 Preheat the oven to 180°C/350°F/ Gas 4. In a large bowl, sift together the flour, cornflour and 50g/2oz/¼ cup of the sugar three times, so the texture is very, very light.

3 Gently fold the sifted flour and the vanilla extract into the whisked egg whites until combined, and transfer to a 25cm/10in non-stick ring mould. Bake for 35–40 minutes until risen and golden. Remove from the oven, invert the cake in its tin on to a wire rack, and leave to cool.

4 To make the frosting, heat the sugar and 60ml/4 tbsp water in a small pan, stirring constantly until the sugar dissolves. Increase the heat and boil until the temperature reaches 115°C/ 240°F on a sugar thermometer. As soon as this temperature is reached, whisk the egg whites until very stiff and dry.

6 Lift the tin off the cooled cake and place the cake on a serving plate or turntable. Spread the frosting over the the cake, using a palette knife to make a swirling pattern.

7 To decorate the cake, sprinkle over the grated orange rind.

COOK'S TIP
This success of this very light cake relies on the care taken during its preparation. It is important to sift the dry ingredients three times and to whisk the egg whites to the right consistency. Make sure you do not overbeat the egg whites. They should form soft peaks, not be crumbly, so that the air bubbles can expand further during the cooking time and help the cake to rise.

VARIATION
For a chocolate version of this cake, replace 25g/1oz/2 tbsp of the flour with unsweetened cocoa powder.

FROSTED CARROT AND PARSNIP CAKE

THE GRATED CARROTS AND PARSNIPS IN THIS DELICIOUSLY LIGHT AND CRUMBLY CAKE HELP TO KEEP IT MOIST AND ACCOUNT FOR ITS VERY GOOD KEEPING QUALITIES. THE CREAMY SWEETNESS OF THE COOKED MERINGUE TOPPING MAKES A WONDERFUL CONTRAST TO THE CAKE'S LIGHT CRUMB.

SERVES EIGHT TO TEN

INGREDIENTS
 oil, for greasing
 1 lemon
 1 orange
 15ml/1 tbsp caster (superfine) sugar
 225g/8oz/1 cup butter
  or margarine
 225g/8oz/1 cup soft light
  brown sugar
 4 eggs
 225g/8oz/1⅔ cups carrot and
  parsnip, grated
 115g/4oz/1¼ cups sultanas
  (golden raisins)
 225g/8oz/2 cups self-raising
  (self-rising) wholemeal flour
 5ml/1 tsp baking powder
For the topping
 50g/2oz/¼ cup caster
  (superfine) sugar
 1 egg white
 pinch of salt

1 Preheat the oven to 180°C/350°F/Gas 4. Lightly grease a 20cm/8in loose-based cake tin (pan) and line the base with a circle of greaseproof paper.

VARIATION
If you do not like parsnips, you can make this cake with just carrots, or replace the parsnips with the same weight of shredded courgettes (zucchini) Add a pinch of cinnamon and nutmeg to the mixture to give a little extra flavour.

2 Finely grate the lemon and orange rind. Put about half of the rind, selecting the longest shreds, in a bowl and mix with the caster sugar. Arrange the sugar-coated rind on a sheet of greaseproof paper and leave in a warm place, to dry thoroughly.

3 Cream the butter and sugar until pale and fluffy. Add the eggs gradually, then beat well. Stir in the unsugared rinds, the grated carrots and parsnips, 30ml/2 tbsp orange juice and the sultanas.

4 Gradually fold in the flour and baking powder, and tip into the prepared tin. Bake for 1½ hours until risen, golden and just firm.

5 Leave the cake to cool slightly in the tin, then turn out on to a serving plate.

6 To make the topping, place the caster sugar in a bowl over boiling water with 30ml/2 tbsp of the remaining orange juice. Stir over the heat until the sugar begins to dissolve. Remove from the heat, add the egg white and salt, and whisk for 1 minute with an electric beater.

7 Return to the heat and whisk for about 6 minutes until the mixture becomes stiff and glossy, holding a good shape. Allow to cool slightly, whisking frequently.

8 Swirl the cooked meringue topping over the cake and leave to firm up for about 1 hour. To serve, sprinkle with the sugared lemon and orange rind, which should now be dry and crumbly.

COOK'S TIP
When this cooked meringue frosting cools, it becomes slightly hard on the outside. The cake will keep well for a few days until the crust is cut into.

HONEY <u>AND</u> SAFFRON BREAD

SWEET BREADS MAKE A GREAT ALTERNATIVE TO PLAIN TOAST FOR BREAKFAST OR TEA. SPREAD THIS BREAD WITH BUTTER WHILE IT IS STILL WARM FROM THE OVEN, OR SERVE AS BUTTERED TOAST.

MAKES TWO 450G/1LB LOAVES

INGREDIENTS
oil, for greasing
flour, for dusting
150ml/¼ pint/⅔ cup, plus
  15ml/1 tbsp milk
several saffron threads
60ml/4 tbsp clear honey
450g/1lb/4 cups plain (all-purpose)
  or strong white bread flour
5ml/1 tsp salt
½ sachet easy-blend (rapid rise)
  dried yeast
3 eggs
60g/2¼oz/4½ tbsp unsalted butter,
  melted and cooled

1 Lightly grease and flour two 450g/1lb loaf tins (pans). Heat half the milk with the saffron in a small saucepan until the colour seeps out of the saffron strands. Stir in the honey and set aside to cool slightly, then add the rest of the milk.

VARIATION
For a richer loaf, add raisins, sultanas (golden raisins) or chopped dried apricots. This rich dough freezes well. Cook the loaves as above for 20 minutes, then reduce the heat to 180°C/350°F/Gas 4 for a further 15 minutes. Remove from the oven, cool, then remove from their tins, wrap well and freeze. To serve, defrost for 2 hours, then bake in an oven preheated to 200°C/400°F/Gas 6 for 15–20 minutes, glazing if necessary.

2 Sift the flour and salt into a large mixing bowl, mix in the dried yeast and make a hollow in the middle.

3 In a separate bowl, beat together 2 eggs plus 1 extra yolk and pour into the flour along with the melted butter and cooled milk. Using a fork, work the egg into the flour until the mixture begins to come together.

4 Turn out on to a lightly floured surface and knead gently until you have a silky, soft, smooth, elastic dough.

5 Return the dough to a clean, lightly greased mixing bowl. Lightly grease the surface of the dough and cover the bowl with a clean cloth. Set aside in a warm place and leave for about 2 hours until doubled in bulk and very spongy.

COOK'S TIP
If you find that you have kept the bread for too long and it has become slightly stale, make into breadcrumbs and store in an airtight container in the freezer. They can be used to make a crisp coating for fish.

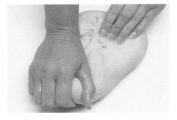

6 Turn the dough out on to a floured surface and knead it well until it is smooth and firm again. Divide into four pieces and shape into smooth round balls. Place them side by side in the prepared tins and set aside in a warm place to double in size again.

7 Preheat the oven to 200°C/400°F/Gas 6. When ready to bake, whisk the remaining egg white and use to glaze the bread. Bake for 35 minutes.

8 Check the bread to make sure it is not browning too quickly, and cover with foil if necessary. Cook for a further 10–15 minutes or until well risen, golden and sounding hollow when tapped underneath. Cool on a wire rack.

GREEK EASTER EGG BREAD

TOPPED WITH BRIGHTLY COLOURED EGGS, THIS ATTRACTIVE PLAITED BREAD IS AN IMPORTANT PART OF GREEK EASTER CELEBRATIONS. THE RED COLOUR USED TO DYE THE EGGS IS THOUGHT TO HAVE MAGICAL PROTECTIVE POWERS.

MAKES ONE LOAF

INGREDIENTS
  oil, for greasing
  450g/1lb/4 cups unbleached
    strong white bread flour,
    plus extra for flouring
  2.5ml/½ tsp salt
  5ml/1 tsp ground allspice
  2.5ml/½ tsp ground cinnamon
  2.5ml/½ tsp caraway seeds
  20g/¾oz fresh yeast
  175ml/6fl oz/¾ cup lukewarm milk
  50g/2oz/¼ cup butter
  40g/1½oz/3 tbsp caster
    (superfine) sugar
  2 eggs
For the coloured eggs
  3 eggs
  1.5ml/¼ tsp red food colouring paste
  15ml/1 tbsp white wine vinegar
  5ml/1 tsp water
  5ml/1 tsp olive oil
For the glaze
  1 egg yolk
  5ml/1 tsp clear honey
  5ml/1 tsp water
For the decoration
  50g/2oz/½ cup split almonds, sliced
    edible gold leaf (optional)

1 Lightly grease a baking sheet. First make the coloured eggs. Place the eggs in cold water, bring to the boil and boil gently for 10 minutes. Lift out of the water and place on a wire rack to dry. Mix together the red colouring, vinegar and water in a shallow bowl, then roll the eggs in the mixture. Return to the rack to cool and dry completely.

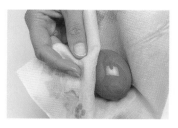

2 When the eggs are cold, drizzle the olive oil on to kitchen paper, lift up each egg in turn and rub all over with the oiled paper.

3 To make the dough, sift the flour, salt, allspice and cinnamon into a large bowl. Stir in the caraway seeds.

4 In a jug, mix the yeast with the milk. In a bowl, cream together the butter and sugar, then beat in the eggs. Add the two mixtures to the flour and gradually mix to a dough.

5 Turn out the dough on to a lightly floured surface, and knead until smooth and elastic.

6 Place the dough in a large lightly oiled bowl, cover with lightly oiled clear film and leave to rise in a warm place for about 2 hours, or until doubled in bulk.

7 Knock back the dough and knead on a lightly floured surface for 2–3 minutes. Return to the bowl, re-cover and leave to rise again in a warm place for about 1 hour, or until doubled in bulk.

8 Knock back the dough and turn out on to a lightly floured surface. Divide into 3 equal pieces and roll each into a 38–50cm/15–20in long rope. Plait these together from the centre to the ends.

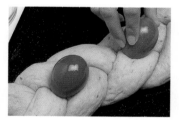

9 Place the dough on the prepared baking sheet and push the dyed eggs into the loaf. Cover and leave to rise in a warm place for about 1 hour.

10 Meanwhile, preheat the oven to 190°C/375°F/Gas 5. Combine the egg yolk, honey and water, and brush over the loaf. Sprinkle with almonds and gold leaf, if using. Bake for 40–45 minutes, or until golden and hollow sounding. Transfer to a wire rack to cool.

HUNGARIAN FRUIT BREAD

THIS RECIPE CAN HARDLY BE CALLED A BREAD AS IT PRODUCES A LOVELY, LIGHT, WHITE CAKE WHICH KEEPS VERY WELL, IF TIGHTLY WRAPPED. IT IS ALSO DELICIOUS SERVED SLIGHTLY WARM AS A PUDDING WITH A RICH PLUM OR FRUIT SAUCE OR EVEN A FRESH EGG CUSTARD.

SERVES EIGHT TO TEN

INGREDIENTS
    oil, for greasing
    7 egg whites
    175g/6oz/generous ¾ cup caster
       (superfine) sugar
    115g/4oz/1 cup flaked (sliced)
       almonds, toasted
    115g/4oz/¾ cup sultanas
       (golden raisins)
    grated rind of 1 lemon
    160g/5½oz/1⅓ cups plain
       (all-purpose) flour, sifted,
       plus extra for flouring
    75g/3oz/6 tbsp butter, melted

1 Preheat the oven to 180ºC/350ºF/ Gas 4 and grease and flour a 1kg/2¼lb loaf tin (pan). Whisk the egg whites until very stiff, but not crumbly. Fold in the sugar gradually, then the almonds, sultanas and lemon rind.

2 Fold the flour and butter into the egg whites. Tip the mixture into the tin, and bake for about 45 minutes until well risen and pale golden brown. Cool for a few minutes in the tin, then turn out and serve warm or cold, in slices.

BLUEBERRY MUFFINS

LIGHT AND FRUITY, THESE WELL-KNOWN AMERICAN MUFFINS ARE DELICIOUS AT ANY TIME OF DAY.
SERVE THEM WARM FOR BREAKFAST OR BRUNCH, OR AS A TEA-TIME TREAT.

MAKES TWELVE

INGREDIENTS
 180g/6¼oz/generous 1½ cups
   plain (all-purpose) flour
 60g/2¼ oz/generous ¼ cup sugar
 10ml/2 tsp baking powder
 1.5ml/¼ tsp salt
 2 eggs
 50g/2oz/4 tbsp butter, melted
 175ml/6fl oz/¾ cup milk
 5ml/1 tsp vanilla extract
 5ml/1 tsp grated lemon rind
 175g/6oz/1½ cups fresh blueberries

1 Preheat the oven to 200°C/400°F/
Gas 6. Grease a 12 cup muffin tin (pan)
or arrange 12 paper muffin cases on a
baking tray.

2 Sift the flour, sugar, baking powder
and salt into a large mixing bowl. In
another bowl, whisk the eggs until
blended. Add the melted butter, milk,
vanilla and lemon rind to the eggs, and
stir thoroughly to combine.

3 Make a well in the dry ingredients and
pour in the egg mixture. With a large
metal spoon, stir until the flour is just
moistened, but not smooth.

VARIATION
Muffins are delicious with all kinds of
different fruits. Try out some variations
using this basic muffin recipe. Replace
the blueberries with the same weight of
bilberries, blackcurrants, stoned cherries
or raspberries.

4 Add the blueberries to the muffin
mixture and gently fold in, being careful
not to crush the berries.

5 Spoon the batter into the muffin tin or
paper cases, leaving enough room for
the muffins to rise.

6 Bake for 20–25 minutes, until the
tops spring back when touched lightly.
Leave the muffins in the tin, if using, for
5 minutes before turning out on to a
wire rack to cool a little before serving.

COOK'S TIP
If you want to serve these muffins for
breakfast, prepare the dry ingredients
the night before to save time.

CURD TARTS

THESE TASTY LITTLE TARTS, FROM THE NORTH OF ENGLAND, HAVE A LIGHT CURD CHEESE FILLING THAT SITS ON A TANGY LAYER OF LEMON CURD.

MAKES TWENTY-FOUR

INGREDIENTS
    450g/1lb shortcrust pastry
    225g/8oz curd (farmer's) cheese
    2 eggs, beaten
    75g/3oz/generous ⅓ cup caster
       (superfine) sugar
    5ml/1 tsp finely grated lemon rind
    50g/2oz/¼ cup currants
    60ml/4 tbsp lemon curd
    thick cream or crème fraîche, to serve

COOK'S TIP
Pastry freezes very well, so save time by lining the tartlet tins with pastry, wrapping them tightly in clear film and storing them in the freezer. When ready to cook, simply remove the tins from the freezer and allow to defrost for 1 hour, then fill and bake.

1 Preheat the oven to 180°C/350°F/ Gas 4. Roll out the shortcrust pastry thinly, stamp out 24 rounds using a 7.5cm/3in plain cutter and use to line patty or tartlet tins. Chill or set aside in a cool place until required.

VARIATION
For special occasions, add a drop of brandy to the filling.

2 Cream the curd cheese with the eggs, sugar and lemon rind. Stir in the currants. Place 2.5ml/½ tsp of the lemon curd in the base of each tartlet case. Spoon on the filling, flatten the tops and bake for 35–40 minutes, until just turning golden.

3 Serve warm or cold, topped with thick cream or crème fraîche.

ALMOND CREAM PUFFS

IN THESE LITTLE PIES, CRISP, FLAKY LAYERS OF PASTRY SURROUND A SWEET, CREAMY FILLING. THEY ARE BEST SERVED WARM, SO REHEAT ANY THAT BECOME COLD BEFORE EATING.

MAKES TEN

INGREDIENTS
275g/10oz puff pastry
15ml/1 tbsp plain (all-purpose) flour, plus extra
2 egg yolks
30ml/2 tbsp ground almonds
30ml/2 tbsp caster (superfine) sugar
a few drops of vanilla or almond extract
150ml/¼ pint/⅔ cup double (heavy) cream, whipped
a little milk, for glazing
sifted icing (confectioners') sugar, for sprinkling

1 Roll out the pastry thinly on a lightly floured surface, and cut out ten 7.5cm/3in rounds and ten 6.5cm/2½in fluted rounds. Keeping the smaller rounds for the tops, use the larger rounds to line a muffin tin (pan). Chill for 10 minutes. Preheat the oven to 200°C/400°F/Gas 6.

2 Whisk the egg yolks with the flour, almonds, sugar and extract. Fold in the cream and spoon into the pastry cases. Brush the edges with milk, add the tops and seal the edges. Glaze with milk and bake for 20–25 minutes until golden. Cool slightly. Sprinkle with icing sugar.

CINNAMON AND ORANGE TUILES

THE AROMA OF CINNAMON AND ORANGE EVOKES A FEELING OF CHRISTMAS AND, SERVED WITH COFFEE, THESE CHOCOLATE-DIPPED TUILES ARE PERFECT FOR FESTIVE OCCASIONS.

SERVES FIFTEEN

INGREDIENTS
  2 egg whites
  90g/3½oz/½ cup caster
    (superfine) sugar
  7.5ml/1½ tsp ground cinnamon
  finely grated rind of 1 orange
  50g/2oz/½ cup plain
    (all-purpose) flour
  75g/3oz/6 tbsp butter, melted
For the dipping chocolate
  75g/3oz Belgian plain
    (semisweet) chocolate
  45ml/3 tbsp milk
  75–90ml/5–6 tbsp double (heavy)
    or whipping cream

1 Preheat the oven to 200°C/400°F/ Gas 6. Line three large baking trays with non-stick baking paper.

2 Whisk the egg whites until softly peaking, then whisk in the sugar until smooth and glossy. Add the cinnamon and orange rind, sift over the flour and fold in with the melted butter. When well blended, add 15ml/1 tbsp of recently boiled water to thin the mixture.

3 Place 4–5 teaspoons of the mixture on each tray, well apart. Flatten out and bake, one tray at a time, for 7 minutes until just turning golden. Cool for a few seconds then remove from the tray with a fish slice and immediately roll around the handle of a wooden spoon. Place on a rack to cool.

4 To make the dipping chocolate, melt the chocolate slowly in the milk until smooth, then stir in the cream. Dip one or both ends of the biscuits in the chocolate and leave to cool.

COOK'S TIP
If you haven't made these before, cook only one or two at a time until you get the hang of it. If they harden too quickly to allow you time to roll them, return the baking sheet to the oven for a few seconds, then try rolling them again.

MINT CHOCOLATE MERINGUES

THESE MINI MERINGUES ARE PERFECT FOR A CHILD'S BIRTHDAY PARTY AND COULD BE TINTED PINK OR GREEN. ANY SPARES ARE DELICIOUS CRUNCHED INTO YOUR NEXT BATCH OF VANILLA ICE CREAM.

MAKES ABOUT FIFTY

INGREDIENTS
  2 egg whites
  115g/4oz/generous ½ cup
    caster (superfine) sugar
  50g/2oz chocolate mint
    sticks, chopped
  unsweetened cocoa powder,
    sifted (optional)
For the filling
  150ml/¼ pint/⅔ cup double (heavy)
    or whipping cream
  5–10ml/1–2 tsp crème de menthe

COOK'S TIP
You can store these meringues in airtight tins or jars; they will keep for several days.

1 Preheat the oven to 110°C/225°F/ Gas ¼. Whisk the egg whites until stiff, then gradually whisk in the sugar until thick and glossy. Fold in the chopped mint sticks and then place teaspoons of the mixture on baking sheets covered with non-stick baking paper.

2 Bake for 1 hour or until crisp. Remove from the oven and allow to cool, then dust with cocoa, if using.

3 Lightly whip the cream, stir in the crème de menthe, and sandwich the meringues together just before serving.

GOLDEN GINGER MACAROONS

*WITH THEIR WARM, SPICY, GINGER FLAVOUR, THESE SLIGHTLY CHEWY LITTLE BISCUITS ARE GOOD
SERVED WITH ICE CREAM AND WILL GO WELL WITH MID-MORNING OR AFTER-DINNER COFFEE.*

MAKES EIGHTEEN TO TWENTY

INGREDIENTS
1 egg white
75g/3oz/scant ½ cup soft light
  brown sugar
115g/4oz/1 cup ground almonds
5ml/1 tsp ground ginger

1 Preheat the oven to 180°C/350°F/
Gas 4. In a large, grease-free bowl,
whisk the egg white until stiff and
standing in peaks, but not crumbly,
then whisk in the brown sugar.

3 Using two teaspoons, place spoonfuls
of the mixture on baking trays, leaving
plenty of space between each. Bake for
about 20 minutes until pale golden
brown and just turning crisp.

VARIATIONS
You can substitute other ground nuts,
such as hazelnuts or walnuts, for the
almonds. Ground cinnamon or mixed
spice could be added to the mixture
instead of ginger for another variation.

2 Sprinkle the ground almonds and
ginger over the whisked egg white, and
gently fold them together.

4 Leave to cool slightly on the baking
trays before transferring to a wire rack
to cool completely.

NUTTY NOUGAT

*THIS CHEWY SWEET IS MADE FROM EGG WHITE WHISKED TOGETHER WITH A HOT SUGAR SYRUP. NUTS
AND CANDIED FRUITS ARE TRADITIONALLY ADDED BUT OTHER FRUITS, SUCH AS DRIED APRICOTS OR
GLACÉ CHERRIES, CAN ALSO BE USED.*

MAKES ABOUT 500G/1½LB

INGREDIENTS
225g/8oz/generous 1 cup
  granulated (white) sugar
225g/8oz/1 cup clear honey or
  golden (light corn) syrup
1 large (US extra large) egg white
115g/4oz/1 cup flaked (sliced)
  almonds or chopped pistachio
  nuts, roasted

1 Line a 17.5cm/7in square tin (pan)
with rice paper and set aside.

COOK'S TIP
If you make this nougat on a very warm
day, you will find it takes longer to firm
up and you will need to wait a little
longer before cutting. It may help to take
it out of the tin as soon as it has set.

2 Place the sugar, honey or golden
syrup and 60ml/4 tbsp water in a large
heavy-based saucepan and heat gently
until the sugar has totally dissolved,
stirring frequently.

3 Bring the syrup to the boil and
boil gently until it reaches the soft
crack stage, or 151°C/304°F on a
sugar thermometer.

4 Meanwhile, whisk the egg white until
very stiff, but not crumbly, then slowly
drizzle the syrup into the egg white
while whisking constantly.

5 Quickly stir in the nuts and pour
the mixture evenly into the prepared
tin. Leave to cool but, before the
nougat becomes too hard, cut it
into squares.

OATY CHOCOLATE-CHIP COOKIES

*THESE CRUNCHY COOKIES ARE EASY ENOUGH FOR CHILDREN TO MAKE BY THEMSELVES AND ARE SURE
TO DISAPPEAR AS SOON AS THEY ARE PUT ON THE TABLE.*

MAKES ABOUT TWENTY

INGREDIENTS
- 115g/4oz/½ cup butter, plus extra
  for greasing
- 115g/4oz/½ cup soft dark
  brown sugar
- 2 eggs, lightly beaten
- 45–60ml/3–4 tbsp milk
- 5ml/1 tsp vanilla extract
- 150g/5oz/1¼ cups plain
  (all-purpose) flour
- 5ml/1 tsp baking powder
- pinch of salt
- 115g/4oz/generous 1 cup
  rolled oats
- 175g/6oz plain (semisweet)
  chocolate chips
- 115g/4oz/1 cup pecan
  nuts, chopped

1 Cream the butter and sugar in a large bowl until pale and fluffy. Add the beaten eggs, milk and vanilla extract, and beat thoroughly.

2 Sift in the flour, baking powder and salt, and stir in until well mixed. Fold in the rolled oats, chocolate chips and chopped pecan nuts.

3 Chill the mixture for at least 1 hour. Preheat the oven to 180°C/350°F/Gas 4. Grease two large baking trays.

4 Using two teaspoons, place mounds well apart on the trays and flatten with a spoon or fork. Bake for 10–12 minutes until the edges are just colouring, then cool on wire racks.

CHOCOLATE TRUFFLES

THESE IRRESISTIBLE AFTER-DINNER TRUFFLES MELT IN THE MOUTH. USE A GOOD-QUALITY CHOCOLATE WITH A HIGH PERCENTAGE OF COCOA SOLIDS TO GIVE A REAL DEPTH OF FLAVOUR.

MAKES TWENTY TO THIRTY

INGREDIENTS
175ml/6fl oz/¾ cup
  double (heavy) cream
1 egg yolk, beaten
275g/10oz plain (semisweet) Belgian
  chocolate, chopped
25g/1oz/2 tbsp unsalted butter,
  cut into pieces
30–45ml/2–3 tbsp brandy
  (optional)
For the coatings
  unsweetened cocoa powder
  finely chopped pistachio nuts
    or hazelnuts
  400g/14oz plain (semisweet), milk or
    white chocolate, or a mixture

1 Bring the cream to the boil, then remove the pan from the heat and beat in the egg yolk. Add the chocolate, then stir until melted and smooth. Stir in the butter and the brandy, if using, then strain into a bowl and leave to cool. Cover and chill for 6–8 hours.

2 Line a large baking sheet with greaseproof paper. Using a very small ice-cream scoop or two teaspoons, form the chocolate mixture into 20–30 balls and place on the paper. Chill if the mixture becomes too soft.

3 To coat the truffles with cocoa, sift some powder into a small bowl, drop in the truffles, one at a time, and roll to coat well. To coat them with nuts, roll the truffles in finely chopped pistachio nuts or hazelnuts.

4 To coat with chocolate, freeze the truffles for at least 1 hour. In a small bowl, melt the plain, milk or white chocolate over a pan of barely simmering water, stirring until melted and smooth, then allow to cool slightly.

5 Using a fork, dip the frozen truffles into the cooled chocolate, one at a time, tapping the fork on the edge of the bowl to shake off the excess. Place on a baking sheet lined with non-stick baking paper and chill. If the melted chocolate thickens, reheat until smooth. All the truffles can be stored, well wrapped, in the fridge for up to 10 days.

EGG INFORMATION AND SUPPLIERS

British Domesticated Ostrich
    Association
33 Eden Grange
Little Corby, Carlisle
Cumbria, CA4 8QW, UK
Tel: 01228 562532
www.ostrich.org

British Egg Industry Council
(BEIC)
www.egginfo.co.uk/knowledge-
    guide

British Egg Information Service
52a Cromwell Road
London SW7 5BE
www.britegg.co.uk

British Goose Producers'
    Association
(part of the British Poultry
    Council)
Europoint House
5 Lavington Street
London
SE1 0NZ
Tel 07725 554944
www.geese.cc

British Nutrition Foundation
Imperial House 6th Floor
15-19 Kingsway, London
WC2B 6UN
Tel: 020 7557 7930
www.nutrition.org.uk

Dr Oetker egg white powder
4600 Park Approach
Thorpe Park
Leeds LS15 8GB
Tel: 0113 823 1400
www.oetker.co.uk/oetker

Duck Producer's Association
High Holborn House
52–54 High Holborn
London WC1V 6SX
Tel: 020 7242 4683
www.duedil.com

Horton Duck Farm
Guildford Road
Rudgwick, Sussex
RH12 3BQ
Tel/Fax: 01403 824070
www.duckeggs.co.uk

International Egg
    Commission
Second Floor
89 Charterhouse Street
London, EC1M 6HR
Tel: (0) 20 7490 3493
www.internationalegg.com

RSPCA Freedom Food
4B Brighton Road, Horsham,
West Sussex, RH13 5BA
Tel: 0300 123 0014
www.rspca.org.uk/freedomfood

Specialist egg producers

Daylay Foods
The Moor
Bilsthorp
Nr Newark
Nottinghamshire NG22 8TS
Tel: 0843 273 1069

Deans Farm (Columbus Eggs)
Bridgeway House
Upper Icknield Way
Tring
Herts HP23 4JX
Tel: 01422 891 811
www.ihertfordshire.co.uk

Stonegate Farmers Ltd
    (Fourgrain Eggs)
15 North Street
Hailsham
East Sussex BN27 1DH
Tel: 01323 846 565

**Free-range and organic
suppliers**

Abel and Cole
16 Waterside Way
Plough Lane
Wimbledon

SW17 0HB
Tel: 08452 62 62 62
www.abelandcole.co.uk

Bushwacker Wholefoods
132 King Street
London W6 0QU
Tel: 020 8748 2061
Chatsworth Farm Shop
Dilsey, Bakewell
Derbyshire DE45 1PP
Tel: 01246 565300
www.chatsworth.org/farmshop

Eastbrook Organic Meat Farm
The Calf House, Cues Lane
Swindon, Wiltshire
SN6 8PL
Tel: 01793 790 460

The Fresh Food Company
326 Portobello Road
London W10 5RU
Tel: 020 8969 0351

McKenzie Bros
Southwood Farm
Southwood Road
Alton
Hampshire GU34 4EB
Tel: 01420 542487

The Game Larder
24 The Parade
Claygate
Surrey KT10 0NU

Tel: 01372 462 879
www.gamelarderclaygate.co.uk

Graig Farm Organics
Dolau
Llandrindod Wells
Powys LD1 5TL
Tel: 01597 851 655
www.graigfarm.co.uk

High Close Farm Shop
Bath Road
Hungerford
Berkshire RG17 0SP
Tel: 01488 686 770
www.thefarmshop.co.uk

C. Lidgate
110 Holland Park Avenue
London W11 4UA
Tel: 020 7727 8243
www.lidgates.com

North Acomb Farm
    Shop
Stocksfield-on-Tyne
Northumberland
NE43 7UF
Tel: 01661 843 181
northacombfarmshop.com

Nutricia
Whitehorse Business Park
Trowbridge, Wiltshire BA14 0XQ
Tel: 01225 711677
www.nutricia.co.uk

The Old Dairy Farm Shop
Path Hill Farm
Reading
Oxfordshire RG8 7RE
Planet Organic
42 Westbourne Grove
London W2 5SH
Tel: 020 7221 7171
www.planetorganic.com

Roseden Farm Shop
Wooperton, Alnwick
Northumberland NE66 4XU
Tel: 01668 217 271

Secretts Farm Shop
Hurst Farm,
Chapel Lane
Milford
Surrey, GU8 5HU
Tel: 01483 520 500
www.secretts.co.uk

Swaddles Green Farm
Hare Lane
Buckland St Mary
Chard, Somerset
TA20 3JR
Tel: 01460 234 591
www.swaddles.co.uk

AUSTRALIA

Australian Egg Industry
    Association
12 Ormonde Parade,
Hurstville
NSW 2220
Tel: 612 9409 6999
www.aecl.org

Australian Poultry Industries
    Association
PO BOX 579
North Sydney
NSW 2059
Tel: 02 9929 4077
Fax: 02 9925 0627
www.agd.com.au

Specialist egg producers

Arrawarra Ostrich Farm
Margaret Withnall
Lot 6,
Alkoomie Place
Wilton
NSW 2571
Tel: 0246545622
www.arrawarrafarm.com.au

David Jones
Gourmet Food
65–77 Market Street
Sydney
NSW 2000
Tel: 612 9266 5544

Farm Pride Foods Ltd
551 Chandler Road
Keysborough
VIC 3173
Tel: 613 9798 7077
Fax: 613 9798 6163
www.farmpride.com.au

Five Star Gourmet Foods
13–16 Willoughby Road
Crows Nest
NSW 2065
Tel: 612 9438 5666

Pace Farms Pty Ltd
Richmond Road
Dean Park
NSW 2761
Tel: 612 9626 9744
Fax: 612 9626 3923
www.pacefarm.com

ACKNOWLEDGEMENTS

The author would like to thank the following for their assistance with the research and historical information: John Farrant at *Poultry World Magazine* and Emma Powell at The Egg Information Service, and also Nicola Fletcher, Christine France, Deh-Ta Hseung, Sue Lawrence, Alan Long, Margaret Shaida and Ruth Watson. The author would also like to thank the following suppliers for their generous loan of props: Divertimenti, 139–141 Fulham Road, London SW3 6SD; Kenwood Ltd, New Lane, Havant, Hampshire PO9 2NH; Kitchen Aid Europa Inc., Brussels, Belgium, c/o Kate Wild, 22 Brackenbury Road, London W6 0BA; Lakeland Ltd, Alexandra Buildings, Windermere, Cumbria LA23 1BQ; Magimix UK Ltd, 19 Bridge Street, Godalming, Surrey GU7 1HY; Tefal UK Ltd, 11–49 Station Road, Langley, Slough, Berkshire SL8 8DR; and Teflon Classics, Classic Housewares Ltd, Imperial Mill, Liverpool Road, Burnley, Lancashire BB12 6HH. All recipe pictures are by Amanda Heywood and all reference pictures are by Steve Moss, except for the following: p6b, The Great Egg Question: Sketches at a Poultry Farm, from *The Illustrated London News*, 2nd April 1887 (engraving) by English School (19th century), Private Collection/ Bridgeman Art Library; p6t, Ms 1175 f59r, Women Buying Eggs (vellum), Vieil Rentier d'Audenarde (1291–1302), Bibliotheque Royale de Belgique/ Bridgeman Art Library; p18 and p19t, The Egg Information Service.

INDEX